NOTHING BUT LOVE:

A Katrina Volunteer Finds

Inspiration in the Aftermath

By J. Baker Young

Copyright Year: 2008

Copyright Notice: by J Baker Young. All rights reserved.

The above information forms this copyright notice:

© 2008 by J Baker Young. All rights reserved.

ISBN 978-0-615-25539-2

Reorder information available at All4Won.com

This book is dedicated to the people of St. Bernard Parish, Louisiana.

ACKNOWLEDGEMENTS

This book would not be possible without the patience and understanding of my husband and children. My trips to New Orleans and St. Bernard Parish were also made possible by my parents and friends who helped my family while I was away. And, of course, by my sister Sandy who took this journey with me. The wonderful Roberta Tenant has my deepest gratitude for her editing services. And the extraordinary people of St. Bernard Parish and New Orleans were, and continue to be, my heroes and my inspiration.

AUTHOR'S NOTE

Every person in this book is real. I changed or omitted some names out of respect for individuals' privacy. But I kept the names of some public figures, government employees, non-profit managers, ministers, friends and family members. If anyone from The Parish recognizes himself or herself in these pages, please know that I haven't forgotten your name. It's written down in my journal and I carry it in my heart. Thank you for inviting me into your homes and lives.

"It is one of the most beautiful compensations of this life that no man can sincerely try to help another without helping himself."

Ralph Waldo Emerson

CHAPTER ONE

Mardi Gras 2008

I never thought I'd see Mardi Gras in New Orleans. To be honest, I never really cared if I did. Don't get me wrong, I've been madly in love with New Orleans since the first time I saw it. I felt as though I'd entered another country without a passport. It was so different from anyplace I'd ever been. But I was not interested in Mardi Gras -- it was too crowded and crazy.

But everything changed in August 2005. An insatiable home-wrecker came to town, wilder than any stripper on Bourbon Street. She tore through the city and left unprecedented destruction in her wake. Six months later, the city was eager to forget her. The residents were still recovering, but they needed something to lift their spirits and remind them of life before Katrina. So they threw a party -- Mardi Gras.

Around the country, people weighed in with their opinions. How could they waste money on a party now? But those who said that didn't know New Orleans. Those of us who did, knew it would bring hope to a place that sorely needed it.

Over halfway across the country, I watched the party from my family room. And for the first time, I ached to be a part of it. This Mardi Gras was more than an opportunity for drunken tourists to stumble through the streets. It was the residents' way of shouting to the world, "We're not dead, and we're not going down without a fight." My attitude toward Mardi Gras had taken a complete 180-degree turn. And I put it at the top of my list of Things To Do Before I Die.

Two years later, I was finally able to cross it off the list. On Mardi Gras weekend my sister Sandy and I stepped off a plane and into sheer bliss. We called our friends Buck and Molly, who are Louisiana natives. They gave us directions to meet them on an elevated stand near Lee Circle. Our mutual friend Johnny had rented the stand and invited the four of us to join him. We watched the Thoth and Bacchus parades, stretching our arms in the air as the sky rained beads. When we weren't catching beads, we were dancing with our arms draped over each other's shoulders. We sang and laughed until our sides hurt. In my mind I was mentally reviewing that List of Things

To Do, crossing off "See Mardi Gras" and writing in "See Mardi Gras again."

Buck couldn't get over the fact that we were on this elevated stand. He kept saying in his Louisiana accent, "You girls don't know how lucky y'all are. Tourists never get to watch the parades from these stands. I've lived here all my life and I've never done this before." But he was wrong about one thing -- Sandy and I did know we were lucky, in more ways than we could count.

We were lucky when we met Buck and Molly two years before this party. And then when we met Johnny about a month later. The three of them live in a suburb about 20 minutes from the French Quarter called St. Bernard Parish. If you saw them at this Mardi Gras celebration, you'd never guess their homes had once been underwater, or that they'd spent the last two and a half years overcoming massive bureaucratic roadblocks to rebuild those homes. You'd never guess how we met them or how we became so close. You'd think they were just average people having a great time. And they were -- sort of.

Buck pulled four beers out of a cooler, handed one to each of us and toasted, "To our best friends from California. If it hadn't been for Katrina, we never would've met you."

****

I went to St. Bernard Parish three months after Katrina to volunteer at a relief center. What I saw and heard shocked, depressed, uplifted and inspired me. I had no way of anticipating the effect it would have. I went back three months later, then one month later, then three months later. And the minute I got on the plane headed home to California, I started planning to go back again. You see where this is going -- something kept drawing me back, and it wasn't the dilapidated buildings and the black mold.

But let's get something straight right from the beginning -- I am not a saint, although I am a Saints fan. I'm just an average woman with a husband and two children. Some days I'm nice and some days I'm not, just ask my daughters. I don't volunteer at soup kitchens or serve on the PTO. In fact, I know a lot of people who volunteer a lot more than I do. But something about St. Bernard Parish reached me at my core -- the residents. When I looked at them in that disaster zone I was struck by a horrifying realization -- *This could be me someday*. And my outlook on just about everything changed.

On my first flight home after Katrina I scribbled frantically in my journal, noting the things I'd seen and the people I'd met. I didn't want to forget anybody's name. I hoped maybe someday I'd be able to find them again to see if their situation had improved. I learned so many important lessons from the people of St. Bernard Parish that I didn't want to forget, and I promised myself I'd pass those lessons on to my children.

As the months went by, my journal got thicker and thicker and one day I realized it had become a book. I knew it was important to save it for my daughters to read when they were older. Because even though I didn't personally experience the lessons that come from living through a disaster, I gained enormous insight from the people who did. Time passed and I still didn't hear much about The Parish in the media. And I was frustrated, because St. Bernard still needed so much help. Word got around in my circle that I'd been doing volunteer work in Louisiana. But when I said I was going to St. Bernard Parish most people asked, "Where?" So I decided it was time to share what I knew with as many people as I could. Because over two years after Katrina, most people still didn't know what had happened in St. Bernard Parish.

They were the Katrina survivors we didn't see on the news. While helicopters in New Orleans were rescuing citizens from rooftops, St. Bernard residents were waiting on their roofs for helicopters that never came. The news reporters didn't show up either. So they swam until they found abandoned boats and then rescued each other from attics and flooded buildings. And then they waited for any kind of help for day after day, with little food or water, in the sweltering heat. New Orleans residents had to wait far too long for outside assistance and St. Bernard Parish residents waited even longer. They called their community "The Forgotten Parish." But to me, and anyone else who went there, St. Bernard was the unforgettable parish.

It sounds cliché to say they changed my life, so I won't say that. I'll just tell you how they did it. And I'll start with this -- the most generous people I ever met were strangers who'd just lost everything.

CHAPTER TWO

The Battle of New Orleans

You may be wondering how I ever found The Parish. It was a fluke, caused by an unexpected change of plans that took place two months before Katrina and the levee breaches performed an unwelcome extreme makeover.

My sister Sandy and I had developed a tradition of taking a long weekend vacation together once a year. A few years earlier we'd chosen New Orleans as our destination. It became our favorite place. We loved the food, the music, the friendly people and their beautiful accents. After that we couldn't think of anyplace else we wanted to visit more, so we kept going back to New Orleans.

We took our third trip there in June 2005. On the final full day of the trip we'd planned on taking a swamp tour, but woke up to pouring rain. We cancelled our plans and lounged around our favorite guesthouse suite, talking and drinking coffee. By early afternoon the rain was gone and we pulled out our travel books to find something else to do. We found a description of the battlegrounds in Chalmette, site of the infamous Battle of New Orleans. It turns out the battle didn't actually take place in New Orleans, it happened just a few miles away in St. Bernard Parish.

I instantly knew I wanted to go there. My sister and I had both been actively involved in troop support, sending care packages to soldiers and Marines in Iraq. We'd received letters and e-mails of thanks, as well as photographs of soldiers with their families before deployment. And we'd developed a soft spot in our hearts for those who fought in current and previous battles. The travel book said the battlegrounds included a cemetery of fallen American soldiers. Sandy and I wanted to go and pay our respects.

On a much lighter note, I'd had a song stuck in my head from the first time we'd planned a trip to New Orleans. It was one I'd learned in seventh grade and it went a little something like this, "In 1814 we took a little trip, along with Colonel Jackson down the mighty Mississip, we took a little bacon and we took a little beans..." The title of the song was "The Battle of New Orleans." Since I couldn't stop thinking of that song, I decided it was time to visit the actual site where the battle had taken place.

We called United Cab for the 20-minute ride to the site. As it turned out, our taxi driver had grown up near Chalmette. When he dropped us off, he told us he'd come back for us when we were done. On the way back to New Orleans, he drove through The Parish and pointed out the school he'd gone to as a child, the street he once lived on, and his cousin's house. It was endearing -- I'd never had a taxi driver who pointed out landmarks from his own life.

Of all the other buildings we passed, the only one that really caught my attention was a church in a strip mall building, Adullam Christian Fellowship Center. I didn't know why it made an impression on me. Except maybe because it was in an unconventional building for a church (a renovated Winn-Dixie) and my church at home was also in an unconventional building. At this point, Katrina was still just a girl's name and nothing more. I had no way of knowing this building would be underwater in two months or that I'd meet the pastor of that church in a relief center.

When Katrina hit I was glued to my TV. I'd come to love New Orleans and had met so many wonderful people from the area. Just like everyone else, I was stunned by what was unfolding on the screen. I knew it was really bad when I saw Anderson Cooper losing his composure as he watched residents sift through the rubble. And then I heard Jeanne Meserve, a seasoned and respected reporter, as she described her experience riding in a boat with a rescue team. She sounded traumatized as she described people pleading for help and animals trapped in trees.

I knew I had to go there to help. I wanted to hop on the first plane allowed to land at the airport. And I was frustrated that driving there was impractical because of the distance. I told my husband and children I wanted to go there. Their response was, "No way! It's too dangerous." My 9-year-old daughter cried and pleaded with me not to go. My husband reminded me of my responsibility to my children, and to keeping myself safe for their benefit. I was resentful to say the least.

I kept the news on all day, day after day. I started feeling sick and I couldn't keep food down and developed chest pains. I went to the doctor. She ran a few tests and told me I had acid reflux, most likely brought on by stress. It seemed unlikely to me. My life wasn't that stressful, except when I watched the news and stewed about my inability to do anything about it.

I saw celebrities on TV traveling to New Orleans to help. I heard all the accolades they received for this -- people called them heroes. I mumbled under my breath, "They're not heroes, they're lucky. Do they have any idea how many of us want to do the same thing but don't have private jets to fly us there?" I was unbearably envious. In an interview, Sean Penn said he'd been fortunate because he was able to get there through the benefit of his celebrity. I smiled with satisfaction knowing at least one of them understood.

Sometimes you hear words of wisdom that stick with you for the rest of your life. Many years before this I'd heard a lecture by Maryanne Williamson, a very gifted writer and speaker. She said something that resonated with me -- that people get the most depressed about a problem in the world when they don't take action to fix it. She said the people who work toward a solution aren't depressed -- they're too busy working. I knew what was causing my poor health and general crabbiness. And I knew it wouldn't get better until I went to the New Orleans area to help. Meanwhile, 90 miles away, my sister Sandy knew the same was true for her.

I watched for reports about the city of Chalmette, where the battlegrounds were located, but heard nothing. All the news reports were about the different parishes -- Orleans Parish, Jefferson Parish. I didn't even know what a parish was, let alone know which one Chalmette belonged to. Finally I searched the Internet and discovered that Chalmette, the battlegrounds, and our taxi driver's hometown were in St. Bernard Parish. I continued to listen for news about The Parish, but there wasn't any. Many days after Katrina made landfall I finally heard a brief news statement, "St. Bernard Parish is underwater." The homes were flooded to the rooftops. Every town in The Parish had been destroyed including Arabi, Chalmette, Meraux, Violet and Poydras. How was that even possible?

I felt a pull not only to go back to New Orleans to help, but to specifically get out to St. Bernard Parish. I wanted to know what happened to that cab driver's childhood home and school. What happened to that military cemetery?

But this wasn't like me. I didn't have much experience with volunteerism. I wasn't one of those people who always jump at the chance to help. But the pull I felt to go to The Parish wasn't just a wanting, it was a knowing. I knew without a doubt I had to go there. I told my family and friends, "I can't not go." But I didn't know why I felt so strongly about it.

Weeks passed and I still had that feeling. Finally, I had a long talk with my husband. I told him that by refusing to acknowledge my need to go he was asking me to be less than who I am. He relented, although he wasn't happy about it. He made me promise not to do anything unsafe and to only go if my sister could go with me. I had to promise to wear boots, gloves and a facemask. He told me over and over, "Just be safe and don't do anything stupid. You have children who depend on you."

I'm one of those people who consider themselves more spiritual than religious. But I had a feeling this yearning to go there was motivated by something bigger than the kindness of my own heart. About a week before my trip there I prayed and meditated. I knew there was a reason for me to go, but I wasn't sure what it was. I asked, "Why do I feel so strongly that I need to go there?" An answer formed in my brain that seemed to come from some other source, because it was something I didn't even believe. The answer was, *To be a witness.* I thought it was ridiculous. My response was, "What is there to witness? Every news station in the country has been covering the area for months. We've already witnessed everything there is to see."

But when I told my friends Nancy and Letty that I was going, both asked me to take pictures to share when I got back because the media coverage had dropped off and they wanted to know what was happening there. So I packed my camera and camcorder just in case I saw something significant.

In the days leading up to that first trip after Katrina, I had a sense of euphoria because I knew it was the right thing to do. I started to feel as if my whole body was buzzing, like I had a strong caffeine high, but I hadn't had any caffeine. I didn't feel fear or trepidation. I had so much energy coursing through me that I felt like I was going to levitate off the ground. I talked to my good friend Barb, who's an ordained minister. She told me, "Some people say when you're on your soul's path, your entire body will vibrate." So I took the strange feelings I was having as an encouraging sign, even though I knew it was weird to feel so happy about going to a disaster zone.

When I look back on it now, it's strange to realize how so many seemingly random pieces came together to lead me to an experience that will stay with me forever. If it hadn't been for that song, that thunderstorm and our soldiers, I never would have gone to The Parish. And if that cab driver hadn't shared so much about his own life, I might not have gone back.

At that time I thought I was going there to help Katrina survivors. But now I know I went there because I needed to learn from them. They helped me believe in the best of the human spirit.

CHAPTER THREE

Dodging a Bullet

In Louisiana, a parish is the equivalent of a county. St. Bernard Parish is a community of small towns that begins just one block from New Orleans' Lower 9th Ward. But St. Bernard isn't part of New Orleans, it's a suburban area of close-knit communities.

People are born and raised in St. Bernard, and they may go away to college, but many of them come back. They teach the children of their high school peers, run the neighborhood grocery store, or work at a local refinery. Some of them commute to New Orleans. There are many extended families in The Parish. So people have dinners on Sundays with their parents and siblings, nieces and nephews. They value family, friends, good times and hard work. They exhibit lots of southern hospitality, but when Katrina came she was an intruder, not a welcomed guest.

The flooding from Katrina began in St. Bernard Parish hours

before flooding began in most of New Orleans. A huge shipping channel leads into The Parish from The Gulf. Katrina's winds pushed a wall of water into that channel that was so tall it overtopped the levees by many feet. Before long those earthen levees disintegrated and collapsed and the water rushed in with such force that houses were knocked off their foundations. St. Bernard Parish became the only county in United States history to ever be completely destroyed by a disaster.

Immediately after Katrina blew through, the news media reported that New Orleans had dodged a bullet. Katrina had taken a sharp turn east at the last minute. They showed people celebrating in The Quarter. There was no word of floodwater in New Orleans yet. But at the same time, residents from St. Bernard Parish had already been stranded on their rooftops for most of the day, because their levees failed while Katrina was still raging in full force.

When Katrina took a sharp turn to the east, she landed on top of St. Bernard Parish. The entire parish of over 500 square miles and 67,000 people flooded to the rooftops in minutes. People barely had enough time to scramble into their attics, where the heat swelled in excess of 100 degrees. In addition, the hurricane spawned tornadoes that tore through neighborhoods, leaving some homes with the second story torn off and the first story completely flooded. But as night fell, the rest of the country still didn't even know what had happened. The people of St. Bernard Parish spent the night in attics and on rooftops, praying that help would come.

A good portion of The Parish was above sea level, and the area was not considered a flood plain before Katrina. Flood insurance was not required for a home mortgage there, as it usually is in flood-prone areas. Therefore, many residents didn't have flood insurance and never anticipated this scenario. Most had homeowners insurance, but insurance companies would later claim they weren't responsible for "wind-driven water damage." Since most homes flooded to the ceiling, people only received insurance money for roofs that had been damaged by Katrina's winds. People whose homes were completely destroyed received insurance money to cover the cost of replacing their roofs and nothing more.

Most of the residents were middle-class, a group the media didn't seem interested in showing in the days after Katrina. I still haven't figured out why they were overlooked. The country and the world were left with the false impression that only the poorest people of New Orleans were struggling, and everyone else was fine.

Walking through The Parish the first time after Katrina was

like walking onto a disaster film movie set. Only it stretched for miles and it was alarmingly real. It was much worse than anything I'd seen on the news and it was overwhelming. All but four homes out of 27,000 had been declared uninhabitable. Every school, business and government building was destroyed. My mind was overloaded by scenes that didn't make sense. Cars were turned over sideways as if someone had attempted a Dukes of Hazzard stunt and failed. People's possessions were littered all over the streets and yards. Ceilings had melted away to expose everything in the attics falling through the spaces between the wood beams. Windows were broken, doors were wide open or broken off. Holes had been punched through the attics as escape routes. The trees had toppled and all the grass and plants were shriveled and brown. In some places the homes had come off their foundations and floated away. Everything was out of place.

I remembered those puzzles I'd viewed as a child called "What is Wrong with this Picture?" In St. Bernard Parish the challenge was to find what was right in the picture. It seemed nothing had been spared -- especially not the people, who had fled to drier cities and were now stranded there because they had no home to come back to. Much of the area looked like a ghost town. It was scary and creepy to see entire cities completely destroyed and no signs of life for block after block. For the residents of The Parish there was no choice but to start over -- whether they could afford to or not and whether they wanted to or not. Fate doesn't always seem to play fairly. Sometimes it looks like a bully who knocks people down with no remorse. When disaster happens, the victims can react with outrage, self-pity, and blame -- or with determination to overcome the fall. Whichever course they choose, they still have to find a way to stand up again.

When I went to St. Bernard Parish three months after the flood, most of the survivors had dusted themselves off, but they were still smarting from the unexpected hit. Many seemed to be in a cloud of shock and grief. Yet there was still a spark of will and spirit that would not be defeated. I saw a woman at the relief center wearing a shirt that read, "I'll Be Back." And there was a brotherly connection between these residents evident in their cheerful greetings, hugs, handshakes and pats on the back.

The relief center I worked at had been organized by a pastor from a local church -- the Adullam Christian Fellowship Center -- the only building I retained a memory of after my first visit to The Parish two months before Katrina. The relief center provided hot meals and supplies to returning residents who had no homes, no electricity, no running water, no stores and no restaurants. Many of the people we met there said, "We lost everything."

But when they'd see each other for the first time since the flood, their eyes would light up and they'd greet each other like long lost friends. In reality, they had been lost friends. Most people from The Parish left prior to the hurricane's arrival, expecting that they'd be back within three days, just like the previous times they'd heeded a hurricane warning. But many were unable to return for over a month, because it took so long for the water to recede. And often friends didn't know where the others had gone to escape. Phone systems were down, and people didn't know how to reach each other. It made my heart ache when I saw them greet each other again. More than once, as I watched their reunions, my eyes would start to water and I'd have to blink it away before anyone noticed.

When I drove through The Parish I saw that people had spray painted the phone numbers where they could be reached on the front of their homes. They also left messages for one another in the spray paint, "Miss Y'All," "We're OK, we're at 504-###-####," "Rick call Kevin." And some people had left words of protest, which included rages and obscenities aimed at Katrina or other entities they felt were to blame, "Kiss our A** Katrina and Levee Board," "You didn't take my pride B****! I'll be back!" I couldn't blame them for the obscenities -- if ever there was a place where cursing should be acceptable, this was it. Some people posted names of their insurance companies and agents with descriptions of how helpful they'd been or not. Even in an abandoned neighborhood, what really mattered was staying connected -- communicating with each other even if they couldn't see or hear each other's responses.

Sandy and I had signed up to work with a relief center where they were preparing and serving hot meals. A cab driver dropped us off early in the morning. But they were getting a late start that day. There wouldn't be much for us to do for a couple hours. I felt frustration welling up inside me. We only had two full days to help out and I didn't want to waste a minute of it.

I asked Sandy to follow me as I walked behind a stack of pallets. I told her, "I didn't come here to just stand around. And I'm getting frustrated. I need to pray because I don't know what to do." She nodded in agreement. We stood behind the pallet and quietly asked for guidance, "Show us where to go and what to do."

We decided to take a walk. We passed a building with a water line on the wall. The line was about five feet above our heads. A few inches below it, another water line. Then another line a few inches lower. It was a chronicle of the times the water had receded and then stopped. We turned a corner and saw flooded-out cars everywhere. They were turned askew with water lines on the windows.

I pulled out my camera because I wanted people to know about this. I filmed the water lines on the building and cars. I talked while I filmed, describing what I was showing. I tried to stay detached, but the dam burst. My voice started cracking as I said the words. "The thing that's just so hard to wrap your brain around is that this goes on for *miles*. All the residents we've talked to, they're so depressed and they say, 'This is going to take years and it's never going to be the same.' And until you see it you say, 'Oh no, it's gonna get better. It'll be better a year from now.' And then when you come out and see this and you see the scope of it, that's what's overwhelming. The *scope* of it...it's ...*huge*. It's gonna take thousands of man-hours to clean this up -- even if you come in and bulldoze it all. It will take thousands of man-hours just to bulldoze everything that's destructed."

We kept walking and wound up in a neighborhood in the town of Arabi. It was destroyed and abandoned for block after block. We learned later that a lot of the residents from this neighborhood were retired. We found one man gutting a house all by himself. A few blocks later, a couple drove by in a truck. The man driving pointed to a house and said, "That was my uncle's house. I used to drive up and down this street on my bike when I was a kid."

One house had been gutted down to the wood frame and all the furniture and property removed, with the exception of about 20 trophies that were proudly displayed on a wooden beam above the front door. Seeing that made us wish we could meet whoever had lived there. We called it The Trophy House and revisited it often on subsequent trips. There was something proud and rebellious about that home.

As we continued walking through the neighborhood, another car drove by. A woman pulled into a driveway and eyed us suspiciously. She must have thought we were looting the neighborhood. Sadly, even if we had been looters, there wasn't much left to take. An ungutted house nearby had even been spray painted with the words, "Looters Welcome." Since it was close to Christmas, Sandy had packed dozens of small candy canes to give to people we met. She approached the woman, telling her she just wanted to give her a candy cane. Then Sandy told her we were looking for ways to help. The woman gave us directions to another relief center a few blocks away.

So that was where we worked. Residents lined up there to get food and toiletries. There was no place in The Parish to buy them. Goods were placed on stacks of pallets that served as makeshift tables. We didn't have any bags for the goods, so people used the leftover boxes the goods had been shipped in.

The residents were all living in tents or FEMA trailers. The most unsettling thing about them was that they looked like people I knew. Some of them reminded me of my parents. And some of them looked like me. It squelched the irrational confidence I'd always had that tragedies like this only happen to other people.

That evening, when Sandy and I returned to our room in The Quarter, I called my husband. He asked about the area. I was still in shock from what I'd seen. I couldn't believe it was possible for this to happen in America. And I had an even harder time accepting that things were still so bad three months after the flood.

In 1989 we'd had a destructive earthquake in Northern California. My husband and I had visited many of the places that had been destroyed by the earthquake -- the Marina District in San Francisco, the Cypress Structure that collapsed on motorists, buildings in Santa Cruz and homes in the Santa Cruz Mountains. I asked Jim if he remembered those places after the earthquake. Then I told him, "Multiply all that destruction by one hundred and that's what I saw today." It wasn't an exaggeration.

I showered and got ready for the evening. Sandy and I had signed up to participate in a 5k walk/run to benefit a local non-profit. It was called Celebration in the Oaks. Since it was December, participants were encouraged to dress in festive Christmas attire. We wore Santa hats and jingle bells. When we got there we saw booths offering free beer for participants before the race. Sandy commented that she'd been involved in a lot of triathlons and marathons, but she'd never been offered free beer at any of those events. A local woman heard her and said, "Then you must not be from around here."

Sandy caught the spirit of the celebration and shared her candy canes with other runners and walkers. She has the gift of spreading laughter and revelry, so this event was perfect for her. But I was still numb from all the things I'd seen that day. The contrast between the destruction in The Parish and the festivity of the benefit left my head in a fog. I felt like I was in a dream.

After the benefit we went to The Quarter to get a drink. I don't usually drink a lot, but that day I understood why some people do. The military presence there was impressive. But it was also a little unsettling to realize the city needed military protection. Most of the patrons were contractors from out-of-state and there were very few women. So we got a lot of aggressive attention in the form of wolf whistles and bad lines. It's amazing how much better looking you get when there aren't any other women around. But the military police stood guard over us, standing right behind us and staring down any men who approached us. It was like having our own personal bodyguards. My family had been so concerned about post-Katrina crime and violence, but I never felt safer in New Orleans than I did that night.

CHAPTER FOUR

Duh

When I came home from that first trip, I was in awe of the residents I had met there and their determination to overcome the worst disaster in our nation's history. I understood that I needed to share what I'd seen. Because most people in our country still didn't have the slightest clue about how bad the situation really was. And even worse, most of them didn't even know St. Bernard Parish ever existed. And I wondered how they could get help if no one knew they needed it.

Way back in 1835, Alexis de Tocqueville said philanthropy is enlightened self-interest. I wasn't deluded enough to think my efforts to help The Parish were based on completely unselfish motives. Seeing The Parish had led me to fear a nightmare scenario in my own community.

My experience in The Parish gave me a glimpse into the factors that influence rescue and relief operations in the wake of a disaster. The first places to receive media attention and help are those most familiar to the rest of the country, regardless of whether or not they've sustained the most damage. Unfortunately, it makes sense. How can media and relief groups deploy to places they've never heard of and know nothing about?

My town is a suburb not far from the cities of Oakland, San Jose and San Francisco. We've been warned for years that we're due for a catastrophic and deadly earthquake. I had never given it much thought, but I guess I expected we'd be rescued if we needed to be. But now the possibility of another outcome haunted me. Would anyone come to help my little suburban town? Or would we be forgotten like St. Bernard Parish?

I felt that by helping people in St. Bernard I was helping myself, because we judge others by our own standards of behavior. If I could help people in St. Bernard Parish, then I could believe someone might help my family if someday we were the disaster survivors. I knew my concern for The Parish was partly motivated by enlightened self-interest.

My sister and I were both determined to tell everyone we could about what we witnessed and try to get more help for the residents. But we were still in shock for the first few days back. Each night for a week I would wake up five or six times from nightmares about The Parish. People would ask me what it was like and I couldn't even talk about it because I was afraid I'd start crying. Finally, four days after I came home, I sat down to write an e-mail to everyone in my address list. It took me hours to write because I kept crying as I typed and remembered. When I was done, the letter was over three pages long. As I was typing, Sandy called and asked what I was doing. When I told her she said, "I just finished doing the same thing."

I wanted people to read that e-mail and be as shocked as I was. I wanted them to understand the urgency and hop on the next plane to Louisiana to help. I sent the e-mail on Friday afternoon. And no one responded. Saturday came, nothing. By Sunday morning I was losing hope that anyone cared at all.

I was turning into an emotional basket case and that kind of pissed me off. And I wasn't even going through PMS or menopause, so I didn't have hormones to blame. I'd always been an emotionally stable person. And to be honest, I'd been a little smug around people who got depressed easily or cried all the time. I just couldn't understand them. I thought they should just snap out of it. Now I was one of them, and it was embarrassing. Here I was having a meltdown and I didn't even live in the Katrina zone. The residents of The Parish had been traumatized far worse than I had, and I hadn't seen any of them wallowing in self-pity.

Sunday morning, a week after my trip, I went to church with my daughters. I thought I'd feel better after. But my mind was preoccupied with trying to find ways to help The Parish. I dropped a copy of the long e-mail I'd written into the collection bag. Maybe my minister would read it and say some really good prayers.

It was almost Christmas, and on the way home one of my daughters started talking about an extravagant gift she wanted. When I told her we wouldn't be able to buy it, she started crying and complaining. I snapped, "I just came from a place where the kids have NOTHING! No toys, no bed, no bedroom, no house! Don't you dare complain to me about what you don't have." Both of my daughters went silent. This is a rare occurrence, so it was a clear sign that they were stunned. Then my 9-year-old asked, "What was the saddest thing you saw?" My voice caught in my throat as I answered, "I saw so many sad things I can't pick just one." People always remember the dysfunctional things their parents did to them. I have a feeling my emotional outburst that day will be something my kids remember for many years.

It is such a helpless feeling to see a horrible situation and not know how to fix it. I felt responsible for sharing The Parish's story, but it seemed like no one was listening. When we got home from church I just wanted to spend the whole day under the covers with the light out. But I knew if I did it would scare my daughters. They'd think mommy had lost her mind. Jim would say he knew I never should have gone there. My sister called. I told her I felt like I just needed to have a little nervous breakdown. She said, "Oh, I already did that, and I highly recommend it. You'll feel better afterward. I'm giving you permission to do it."

So when Jim and the kids were busy in the house, I snuck out to the garage, locked myself in my car and had a good cry. Then I started yelling at God: "What good does it do for me to witness something if I tell people and it falls on deaf ears? Nobody cares! It's Your responsibility, not mine, You do it. You find people who will listen. You find someone who will care and do something about it." I raged and cursed. I'm not proud of it. I'm probably lucky I wasn't struck by lightning.

Then I went back in the house, opened my e-mail and found a response from my friend Sue. She'd read my message to her family and they were discussing what they could do to help. It was the first positive response I'd seen, and it was the little bit of encouragement I needed to keep trying.

My father told me I should write to the local news stations and tell them I had video footage of the area. So on Sunday evening I sent messages to three local stations begging them to cover St. Bernard Parish. I didn't really expect to get a response, but it couldn't hurt to try. On Monday morning I had a reply from CBS news station KPIX in San Francisco, "We're interested. Can you be available for an interview?"

I was ecstatic and terrified at the same time. I'm a shy person by nature. The thought of being interviewed on TV was scary, but it'd be worth it if it would help The Parish. I sent them a copy of the long e-mail I'd sent to friends, to more thoroughly explain what was happening in St. Bernard Parish. They interviewed me that day and aired the interview with some of the video footage I'd taken. And they posted my long e-mail message on their website.

I could almost hear God having a good chuckle. Hadn't I told Him to find people who would listen?

CBS 5: Katrina Aftermath: A Bay Area Woman's Journal:

It is Friday and I just returned home from a trip to New Orleans. I am haunted by what I saw there. My sister and I have taken a trip to New Orleans every year for the past three years. We call it our Sister-Bonding weekend. Our last trip was in June 2005. When we saw the devastation of Hurricane Katrina and the broken levees we knew we had to go there to help. But family and job commitments delayed our trip. We wouldn't be able to go until December. I was anxious to get there and concerned there wouldn't be anything left for us to do by the time December rolled around. It was a needless worry -- it turned out there was too much for us to do. But one thing we can do is tell the story of what has happened there and share what still needs to be done.

The French Quarter looked good, as we expected. It was still a place to go for good food and music and to watch people get crazy and laugh. But the taxi driver who picked us up at the airport could barely fit our luggage in his trunk because he had his own suitcase and sleeping bag inside. He told us his first floor apartment had been flooded and he was sleeping in his car until the repairs were completed.

We arrived in New Orleans late Friday afternoon with plans to work at a relief center in St. Bernard Parish the following morning. When we told people in The Quarter about this, they'd shake their heads and say, "Prepare yourselves, it's bad out there," "Did you bring breathing masks? You're going to need them," and "God bless you for what you're going to do." I asked a local if it was as bad as it looked on the news. He told me it was worse, because on the news you only see one frame at a time. When you're there you see destruction all around you.

THE DAMAGE
The next morning we took a taxi out to St. Bernard Parish. In Louisiana, a parish is the equivalent of a county. We passed the Bywater, the Lower 9th Ward, and the cities of Arabi and Chalmette. I took my video camera and filmed through the window. We couldn't believe what we saw -- miles and miles of destruction, 360 degrees around us, as far as our eyes could see. It's hard to describe it. It is one of those things you have to see to fully understand.

Imagine driving through a city in which not one building has survived. Every home, every business is uninhabitable. That is what happened in St. Bernard Parish. Abandoned cars are everywhere, with the water marks from the flood up to the tops of the windows. The door to every building is wide open, windows all broken. Sofas are sticking out of windows, refrigerators on top of houses, tool sheds are overturned or resting in the tops of trees. Debris is everywhere. Ketchup bottles, insulin bottles, CDs, award ribbons, clothes, shoes, and toys are stuck in the dried mud around every home. And this is three and a half months after the storm and flood. Our taxi driver told us the area has been cleaned up a lot. "You should have been here a few weeks ago," he says. We saw a house that has come off its foundation and now rests in the street. He says that happened to many houses, but the work crews have cleaned up the streets so now cars can pass through them.

The previous night in the French Quarter a military policeman told us the soldiers who'd come there from the war said this area looked worse than Iraq. A number of people told us St. Bernard Parish looked like a war zone. I thought it must be a dramatic exaggeration until I saw it for myself. Now I think I know what an American city would look like if it were struck by an atomic bomb -- destruction everywhere, and hardly any people. It looked like a ghost town.

We took a walk through an Arabi neighborhood. This neighborhood had flooded to the rooftops. We talked to a man who was there gutting his friend's house. He said it had been a nice middle-class neighborhood. We could see the remnants of homes that had been lovingly cared for -- beautiful fountains and expensive doors and light fixtures. We peeked inside the homes, which was easy to do because all the doors were wide open or torn off. Piles of insulation had fallen from the ceilings and lay on top of overturned furniture. Carpet no longer sat neatly on the floor -- it was crumpled up into a mound with furniture and dishes strewn on top of it. Everything was filthy from stewing for weeks in what was effectively sewer water. In some houses the sheetrock had melted off the walls. And the walls that had sheetrock were covered in mold.

I saw an overturned couch on a kitchen counter, a boat on someone's lawn, a wooden tool shed turned over with the door pointed to the sky. I saw a refrigerator with the doors broken off lying on a rooftop, with a deer lawn decoration sitting inside it, and a children's plastic picnic table next to it. And this was just one neighborhood. I knew from our cab ride that the entire parish looked like this. Several people told us the towns further down the road were even worse.

The thing that overwhelmed me the most was the massive scale of destruction. It goes on for so many miles that we never saw the end of it. I looked at the damage and commented that it would take hundreds of thousands of man-hours to clean up these homes, businesses and neighborhoods. Our cab driver, who appeared to be in his 50s, commented, "It won't be completed in my lifetime."

I repeatedly asked, "Why aren't we seeing this in the news?" Everyone answered, "People are tired of hearing about it." But I disagreed. When I told friends I was going to help in New Orleans many of them asked me to take pictures and call them as soon as I came home because they wanted to know how the area was doing. A number of people commented that we'd been inundated with information about the area in the initial stages, but now very little is reported about the survivors.

THE LITTLE RELIEF CENTER THAT COULD
We found the relief center where we'd planned to help. But after half an hour there we became frustrated because hardly any work was getting done and we felt we were wasting valuable time. So we walked a few blocks to another relief center, in the parking lot of a flood-damaged Wal-Mart, behind a FEMA tent. We saw volunteers serving hot meals to residents and giving away used clothing, canned goods and toiletries. We told them we wanted to volunteer and they said, "Great, we can always use volunteers. Just start emptying boxes and putting goods out on the tables for the residents to take." And that is what we did for the next two days.

All day long a steady stream of residents came here to get supplies they needed. There are no stores for many miles, so this was their only source for necessities. Some of the residents, the lucky ones, lived in FEMA trailers. Others had moved temporarily to other cities and came back to try to clean and gut their houses. Most of the homes here still had no running water or electricity.

The group we volunteered with was called PRC Compassion. It is composed of many churches throughout the country that want to support the Katrina survivors. The relief center was led by Pastor Glen, who was from a local church in The Parish. His church and home were destroyed in the flood. But he was rebelliously upbeat and positive. He worked as hard as anyone else, driving a forklift and unloading donated items from trucks. He said he'd been doing this work for five weeks and intended to keep on doing it.

One of the other volunteers told me the items we were distributing on this day came mostly from shelters on the Gulf Coast that were closing because the residents there had found other accommodations. PRC Compassion had sent trucks to those shelters to take their unused donations to St. Bernard Parish for distribution.

This relief center was the only place where we saw a flurry of people and activity. My sister and I and four volunteers from Indiana raced around unloading pallets of goods and placing them on makeshift tables. There were so many people in need it was hard to keep up with the demand. But none of the residents were greedy. They asked politely, "May I take two cans of green beans? I have a work crew to feed." I took a mental inventory of the items we gave away: dried beans, rice, canned fruit, pineapple juice, macaroni and cheese, corn bread mix, fresh apples, canned green beans, Veg-all, tomato sauce, small packs of coffee, protein bars, snack packs of pudding, saltine crackers, toothbrushes, antibacterial hand gel, shampoo, soap, sanitary napkins, adult diapers, baby diapers, baby food, formula, trash bags and -- most treasured of all -- bottled water and bleach. We received a case each of toilet paper and paper towels. And although each resident took only one pack, the paper supplies were depleted within five minutes.

There was such a demand for bottled water that we had to assign a limit -- two bottles per person. These weren't the big gallon bottles; these were the size you carry around when you're exercising. Someone asked, "Can I have a little more water? I have no running water and I need to clean my house." I told them to take what they needed. I knew I wasn't supposed to, but I kept telling people to take more water if they need it. Luckily, we didn't run out.

The residents in line were mostly middle-class and many of them reminded me of my own friends and family. It was a sobering reminder that in my home state of California we are just one big earthquake away from walking in their shoes. They expressed so much gratitude for the smallest comfort items. Many of them said to me, "Thank you so much for being here." I felt like a fraud. I was there for one weekend to provide small comfort and then I would go home to my warm house and my closet full of clothes while they stayed here to rebuild with no heat, no plumbing, and no possessions. The only thing I could think to say back to them was, "This is the least we can do."

The previous night in The Quarter we talked with a group of contractors from out-of-state who were working on the underground gas lines in St. Bernard Parish. One of them kept heaping praise on us for coming to New Orleans to volunteer. He said the volunteers and the military working in the area are the heroes. But he felt like "a whore" because he came there for the money. Working at the relief center I didn't feel like a hero at all -- I felt grossly inadequate.

People came to me to ask for items they needed but we didn't have: mops, brooms, cleaning supplies, face masks, toothpaste, toilet paper, blankets, diapers in size 1, 2, or 4 (we only had size 3). In the two days we were there we ran out of antibacterial hand gel, coffee and bleach. It was such an awful feeling to tell someone, "I'm sorry, we don't have diapers for your newborn baby."

THE ELDERLY WOMAN
Every resident of New Orleans and its surrounding

communities had a personal story that would break your heart. Even those who still have homes have either lost their jobs or customers, or are missing their friends who've been forced to move away. They say 80% of the residents lost their homes. In St. Bernard Parish the toll was higher.

One Chalmette resident who still works for the City of New Orleans told us he slept in a ticket booth at a rodeo grounds for the first couple weeks after the hurricane. Then he upgraded to a horse trailer. His in-laws live in Louisiana, and he stays with them when he can make the commute. When he can't, he still sleeps in the horse trailer.

At the PRC Compassion relief center I noticed an elderly lady with a small box making her way through the line. She was limping badly. When she reached the end of the line I told her I'd carry her box to her car. On the way to her car she told me she was 83 years old. She was living in a hotel in New Orleans, but was supposed to get a FEMA trailer in two days. The only problem was that she needed to clear the debris from her property before FEMA would bring a trailer. She says, "I just had my flu shot today and my doctor told me to go home and rest, so I can't clean the debris today." I'd seen the amount of debris in the neighborhoods here, and as I watched this woman limp to her car, I knew she wouldn't be able to clean the debris on a good day. She told me she has four sons who live in other areas and can't or won't come to help her. Her face became sad and she said, "Sometimes when you raise children you get disappointed."

When we arrived at her car I noticed it was filled with things like clothes, a few pairs of shoes, bananas and other food items. I thought to myself, "This looks like a homeless person's car." And then I thought, "*Duh*, she *is* a homeless person." I told her if she gave me her name and phone number I would pass it on to Pastor Glen and see if he knew someone who could help her. She seemed pleased about this and gave me her information. Later I told Pastor Glen about her and he said he would put her at the top of his list. But he looked defeated. He said there just aren't enough volunteers to help everyone. He hopes to help a lot of residents with work like this, but on many days he has no more than seven volunteers. And it takes that many to run the relief center.

There are so many more personal stories I'd like to share. But I'd be writing for another five or ten pages. One thing just about everyone mentioned was they are afraid. Hurricane season will be back in six months. They don't know if the levee breaches will be repaired in time. And if they are repaired, they still may only be strong enough to withstand a category 2 hurricane. The people of New Orleans and St. Bernard Parish asked us to tell people what is going on there. And they said to please, please write to Congress and urge them to provide funding and labor to repair the levees.

One woman we met lives five blocks from a levee, on the opposite side of the breach. She said she's terrified that the next time her side of the levee will breach. If it does, her house will flood to the rooftop. Will she be able to get to the roof in time? And will anyone come to help her?

There are many ways the public can help the people of New Orleans. We can share their stories and repeat their stories, write to Congress, visit New Orleans to support the businesses, volunteer at a relief center, or donate to a relief organization. I can say with certainty that PRC Compassion is making a difference and getting donations to the people. But they need more volunteers and more items.

Before long I saw more and more people become involved in efforts to rebuild New Orleans and The Parish. It wasn't always on a large scale, but even small contributions made a difference.

After Katrina, there was a lot of focus on the bad things people did. But what I experienced only reinforced my belief that people are basically good. Millions of people donated to relief organizations and many countries offered support. Even the residents affected by Katrina helped each other and supported the volunteers.

Before I went on that first Katrina relief trip, my friend Teresa handed me a batch of her famously delicious toffee to take to the owners of the guesthouse in New Orleans. She couldn't physically go there to help, but she could offer something from the heart that she knew she did well. She included a note with a message of encouragement, and it made the guesthouse owners so happy. My other good friend Nancy gave me three handmade baby quilts. They were beautiful and made, like Teresa's gift, with a thoughtful heart. I gave those blankets to parents at the relief center, and you'd have thought I'd given them gold. Word got out, and for the rest of the day parents and grandparents came to the center to ask for quilts for their babies.

For more than a year, people surprised me with their generous contributions. My children's school collected supplies for the one school that had reopened in The Parish to serve the needs of 15 flooded schools. Our local preschool collected socks, toothpaste and toothbrushes for the relief center. At Christmastime, my daughter's 5th grade class sponsored a single mother with four teenage daughters in The Parish.

Our church collected donations for two charities helping The Parish. And the children at church held a bake sale to raise money for the St. Bernard Parish Animal Shelter. One day our minister announced that she'd received a phone call from one of the charities. The woman who called thanked Rev. Mary Anne for the money. But she said the thing they were most grateful for was the fact that we hadn't forgotten them. At the one-year mark, Rev. Mary Anne Harris devoted the entire service to the Katrina anniversary. She asked if Sandy and I would speak to the congregation about The Parish. She also called a local newspaper. A few days later The Tri-Valley Herald ran a front-page story, quoting what we'd said in church that day. We held on to hope that people would help if they really understood.

My good friend Letty was a cheerleader through all my efforts to raise awareness about The Parish. She approached her children's school and her son's basketball team for donations to charities in The Parish. At Christmastime, in 2006, Letty organized a Christmas party for a group of mothers from the school. She'd done the same thing the previous year and asked everyone to bring something small for a gift exchange. But this time she asked everyone to bring a gift for a family in The Parish with two young sons. She said, "I don't want to have a gift exchange among ourselves this year, we all have enough. I want to help someone from St. Bernard." The women responded enthusiastically, and brought piles of toys and gift cards. They felt happier giving these gifts than they had when they received gifts the year before.

My parents were a huge source of support, too. They'd listen to my long stories about The Parish and encourage me to keep trying to get help. Every time I went to The Parish, they picked my children up from school and stayed with them until my husband came home from work. And they even babysat my dog.

My sister Sandy was the only person who knew exactly how I felt. We'd spend hours on the phone together, remembering and brainstorming. She has always been the brave one in our family. But having her with me on those trips inspired me to be brave too. She also became involved in many projects to raise donations and awareness for The Parish.

At first, my husband and my daughters didn't understand why I was so obsessed with The Parish. But they stood by me anyway, and I'll never forget that. Jim had the burden of holding down the fort while I was away. And my daughters had to deal with the uncomfortable feeling a child has when her mother's away. But, in time, the three of them came to love The Parish too. I'll tell you more about that later.

But the kindness that surprised me the most, was the kindness extended to me and my family by the residents of St. Bernard and New Orleans. Because they were the ones who lost everything, but it seemed they were always offering to help us.

CHAPTER FIVE

I Don't Like Spiders and Snakes

I was trying to convince other people to go to the The Parish, and in the process I convinced myself to go back. The first time I went to The Parish I didn't know why I felt so compelled to go. But this time I did. The images were burned in my brain. For all I knew, that 83-year-old woman was still waiting for someone to help clear the debris from her property. And there were thousands of other people like her.

The national media focus was still on other areas affected by Katrina, so those places attracted the most volunteers. I kept screaming at my TV, "What about St. Bernard Parish?" Every time I saw a news report about Katrina the reporters were standing in the Lower 9th Ward. I'd seen the Lower 9th, and it was in bad shape. But it covered an area of about two square miles. St. Bernard Parish had an equal degree of devastation for 500 square miles. I wanted the Lower 9th Ward to get help, but I wanted St. Bernard to get help too. I e-mailed national TV news and talk shows. But none of them expressed an interest in telling St. Bernard's story. I remembered the words Gandhi is famous for, "Be the change you wish to see in the world." The change I wished to see was an increase in the number of volunteers. And the only way to be that change, was to be one of those volunteers. So I made plans to go back.

But I didn't know I'd end up having fun while I was there or that I'd be treated so well. We've all heard about Southern Hospitality. But I didn't expect to find it in a place where people didn't have living rooms or kitchens. I was wrong.

Three months after the first post-Katrina visit, Sandy and I were on a plane headed for New Orleans again. One of Sandy's friends wanted to help too, so we met her at the New Orleans airport.

We planned to work with the PRC Compassion relief center again. Sandy contacted Adullam Christian Fellowship Center and learned that Pastor Glen had been called to a mission outside the country. Pastor Randy would be our contact person at the relief center this time.

We'd already seen the cities of Arabi and Chalmette, on the western end of The Parish. But I felt an intense pull to see some of the cities further east. Several people told us the cities of Meraux and Violet had severe damage. I couldn't imagine how they could be worse than Arabi and Chalmette.

We'd also heard there'd been a big oil spill on the eastern side of Chalmette. When the floodwater plowed through, it picked up a storage tank of crude oil at a local refinery. The tank lost its structural integrity and leaked, causing the largest residential oil spill in United States history, which affected 1,500 homes. The unfortunate residents who lived near the refinery on the eastern end of Chalmette came back to homes destroyed not only by water, but also by oil. I wanted to see this area for myself. Most of the country didn't even know about this. How was that possible? I felt the people who'd been affected deserved to be seen and acknowledged.

There was also some good news in The Parish. Home Depot had reopened a store there shortly before our second trip. I'm sure the decision was based on the potential for huge profits in an area that had to be completely rebuilt. But it doesn't matter. Their decision to reopen helped launch rebuilding projects all over The Parish. Most people couldn't even start rebuilding until there was a place to buy the supplies they needed. Their tools had been washed away in the floodwater, so they were starting from scratch. The Home Depot building was so damaged that the store could only operate in the outdoor garden center. But it wasn't filled with plants. Instead, the shelves were stocked with hammers, saws and building materials.

I tried to think of a way to support residents in their return to The Parish, and it seemed like giving out Home Depot gift cards might be a good way to do that. I couldn't afford to give much, but maybe even a small amount could be helpful. So I purchased some $25 gift cards, and when my parents heard about it they gave me money to buy more. Then my friend Letty bought some too.

The PRC Compassion relief center was still operating in the Wal-Mart parking lot. Wal-Mart was still closed, as were almost all the other national chain stores and restaurants. But we were encouraged to see there were more volunteers at the center this time. A few hours into our first day, a group of high school students arrived to volunteer. There were so many of us, we were practically in each other's way. I saw it as the perfect opportunity to step away for a little while and explore The Parish.

So I decided to take the rental car and go off on my own, hoping I'd get a chance to distribute the gift cards. Taking off on my own in an unfamiliar place was totally out of character for me, but I felt I had to see more. And I was learning to follow my instincts.

When I came home in December, I woke up five or six times each night from nightmares about The Parish. But, as the days went by, I could only remember one of those nightmares. In the dream, I was helping someone gut her house when a snake suddenly slithered out of the debris and bit me. As I started to pass out from the venom, I thought to myself, "Oh, damn! There aren't any hospitals around here anymore!" Later, when I remembered my dream, I had to laugh at myself because I was pretty sure they didn't even have snakes in The Parish.

Three months later I was back. I drove away from the relief center, headed for the town of Meraux. It wasn't hard to find. As I drove past an oil refinery, I noticed a water tower ahead with the word Meraux painted on it. I turned on a residential street, hoping to find people working on houses who might be willing to take a gift card. But I was a little nervous. I didn't want to insult anyone. But then I met Mr. Williams. He told me he had owned six homes -- one he lived in, and five he rented. "I lost all of them," he said.

He was talking with another man as they each took a short break from gutting homes. I stopped my rental car to ask if they were rebuilding. Mr. Williams said he was, so I handed him a Home Depot gift card. He said, "Thank you! Give him one too!" and pointed at his neighbor. He made me laugh. He was grateful, but he wanted to make sure I helped his friend, too.

He was 65, retired and had been living on social security and the income from his rental properties. The home he lived in was in the oil spill zone in Chalmette. He didn't anticipate ever being able to move back to it. And the amount of money the oil company was offering as compensation wasn't enough for him to purchase a new home. He said he applied for a small business loan to repair his rentals. The people at the SBA were very nice to him and told him they'd do everything they could to get his loan approved. But when the final decision was made, the loan was denied. They said he didn't have enough income to support the loan. He protested, "But the houses *were* my income!"

The three of us talked for so long that I ended up turning the engine off so I wouldn't waste gas. The other man had moved out of the area and came back to Meraux to gut his house. Mr. Williams didn't actually come from this neighborhood. His daughter's home was there. He said she'd relocated to Texas for her job and he was gutting and repairing her home. He was living in the backyard in a FEMA trailer with his 92-year-old mother.

After about 20 minutes of talking he said, "Pull your car over and come see the house." He was the first of many St.

Bernardians to say that to me. I thought he seemed OK, that it was probably safe. But I also knew if he turned out to be an axe-murderer everyone would say, "How could she have been so stupid?"

I got out and he showed me how he'd gutted the house down to the wood frame. It had been a pretty house from what I could see. He and the other man in the neighborhood said hardly anyone was rebuilding all the way. They were just gutting down to the frames. They didn't think it made much sense to bring in sheetrock when the levees were still being repaired, and the possibility of another flood loomed with the hurricane season only three months away.

I'd realized that the more time I spent in The Parish, the less shocked I was by all the destruction. I asked Mr. Williams if he'd grown accustomed to seeing all the destroyed buildings around The Parish. He said, "No, every time I step out of my trailer and look around I feel sick again."

As I was leaving, Mr. Williams told me about other neighborhoods I should see. He asked if I'd seen the shrimp boat. When I said I hadn't, he described a shrimp boat that had floated at least two miles inland and landed in a residential neighborhood. It was still there six months after the flood. He gave me directions to the location, but I got lost and turned a few blocks too early.

I wound up in a neighborhood of beautiful custom homes that had been ravaged by the flood. I later learned it was the Lexington Place subdivision, one of the nicest in The Parish. It was situated next to a canal that had breached.

I saw a woman close to my age outside her home, so I asked if she was rebuilding and gave her a gift card. Her name was Diane. Just like Mr. Williams, she invited me in to see her house. It had been gutted down to the frame, but I could still see that it had been a really nice one-story home.

She told me her husband hadn't wanted to leave when the hurricane was coming. But the neighbors were all evacuating. All the TV reports were warning people that this could be the hurricane they'd all feared -- one that might cause extensive flooding in New Orleans. People in St. Bernard weren't sure what that might mean for them, but most didn't want to take any chances. One neighbor with a two-story home gave Diane the key to his house in case there was a flood. And another neighbor offered his boat because he was concerned too. When she saw the neighbors' concern, she told her husband they had to leave, and they did. It was a wise decision because their neighborhood flooded to the rooftops, and they had two children.

I was surprised by what she said next. She thought the flood had been good for her children. She explained her belief that children are materially spoiled today. Diane admitted her own children had been too. By the looks of her house and this nice neighborhood, it wasn't that hard to imagine. But she told me she'd always told her kids they should appreciate what they had because one day it could all be taken away. When Katrina and the flood wiped out everything she told them, "This is what I meant." She said it was a hard lesson for her children, but in the long run they would be better people because of it.

She took me out to her backyard and showed me her pool. It had beautiful tile details around the top, but I couldn't see the bottom because it was filled with brown murky water. I stepped close to look into the water and she said, "Don't get too close, there are snakes in that pool. We've seen them."

I took a big step backward as I continued to look into the water, and I noticed a bunch of little brown guppies. I couldn't believe it. "You have fish in your pool?"

"Well yeah, honey, there's no telling what's in that pool. You can't see the bottom. There could be a dead body in there for all we know."

I started to laugh at what I thought was a joke but she said, "I'm serious. They're still finding dead bodies around here."

I asked her about the snakes. She said they were probably water moccasins that were carried in from a nearby marsh when the floodwater passed through.

I noticed her fence was missing and I could see right into her neighbors' yards. She told me she had a beautiful cedar fence, but the floodwaters carried it away. And there was no trace of it anywhere.

Diane told me her family planned to rebuild their home and sell it, but many neighbors hadn't even begun to gut their homes. She pointed at a nearby two-story house as an example of a home that hadn't been touched since the flood. She encouraged me to peek through the wide-open front door. She told me the refrigerator was still in there with rotting food inside. I could see a few feet of dried dead marsh grass covering the floor from wall to wall. And there was overturned furniture everywhere. She told me, "Don't step inside, there are probably snakes in there too."

Not far away, a neighbor had spray painted the word "SNAKES" in front of his boarded up home as a warning to any potential looters.

As I prepared to leave she hugged me and said, "God bless you." She thanked me for the gift card. I apologized that it wasn't for a larger amount. It was so little compared to the amount it was going to cost them to rebuild.

She answered, "Well this is $25 more than I had before. I'm going to Home Depot right now to buy a hose and a shovel."

She pointed down the block and told me to drive by the street closest to the levee, to see where all the houses had been knocked off their foundations by floodwater. I drove around the neighborhood and saw that the houses had washed away. On some properties the only thing left was a slab foundation and a pile of debris. Remarkably, the toilets were still attached to the foundations, but nothing else.

I turned a corner and continued driving past more destroyed homes. Some that were still standing had debris piles pouring from the windows, as if the houses had vomited their contents. I turned another corner and gasped because I saw a one-story brick house in the front yard of a two-story house. I'd seen a photograph of these houses online, but it was overwhelming to stumble across them unexpectedly in real life. No one else was around and it was scary to be alone in the middle of this disaster area. It felt like I was the only person left at the end of the world.

When I'd seen a photo of these homes, I'd imagined the brick house must have been removed shortly after the flood. But it still sat there, as if the floodwaters had just receded. The foundation was still attached to it -- it looked as though it had just popped out of the ground and floated away in one piece. The strangest thing about it was that I couldn't find a missing house across the street or on either side of the two-story house. Where had that brick house come from? I took a picture and a quick video clip, because I couldn't believe what I was seeing. I guess I thought I could make sense of it later if I just looked at it long enough.

After a while, I realized I'd been away from the relief center for almost two hours. I headed back to pick up Sandy and her friend. I told them about the brick house and they looked at me as if I was crazy. When I told them it hadn't come from across the street or next door they scoffed. Of course it had, I must be mistaken.

The next day I took Sandy with me out to the same neighborhood so she could see it for herself. On our way, we drove down Judge Perez Drive, one of the busiest streets in The Parish. We noticed throngs of people standing on the sides of the road and realized they were getting ready for a parade. They looked so happy. It was incredible to see them celebrating, when we knew every resident had lost his home to the flood just over six months earlier. And The Parish still looked like someone had dropped a bomb on it. We wondered how they'd found the spirit to celebrate in such dire conditions.

I took Sandy to the Lexington neighborhood and showed her the brick house that had moved in front of another house. Then I took her to see Diane's home too. One of her neighbors was there working on his own house. He saw us and introduced himself as Joe. He was the neighbor who'd offered his boat to Diane before he evacuated.

Joe took us into his house and showed us the water line left by the flood. It was six inches above the second story floor. He told us his son was a Marine who'd recently served in Iraq. Joe had gutted the first floor of his home down to the wood frame, and was in the process of working on the second story. It looked like he'd done all the work on his own, pushing each wheelbarrow full of destroyed belongings to the curb. It wasn't uncommon to see men working alone on their homes because their friends and extended families were all busy rebuilding their own homes. Their wives were often in other cities -- keeping up the house, apartment or trailer the family was temporarily calling home.

Joe, like many other people there, told us the Mississippi River Gulf Outlet had been responsible for flooding The Parish. It was a federal project, one the residents had resisted when it was built in the 1960s because they were afraid it would lead to flooding. They'd been right. Now the residents were hoping Congress would vote to close the MRGO, to spare them from future floods. Many people were afraid to rebuild if it remained open.

Joe also told us the insurance companies weren't paying much. He said his insurance company was only paying for about 10% of the damages to his home. This was a problem all over St. Bernard, and in the other areas of Louisiana that had been damaged by Katrina. For many families, that was the biggest factor in the slow recovery process. Imagine trying to rebuild your house with only the money you have in your checking and saving accounts. How long do you think it would take? In later visits I would meet a man who said he had tripled his debt to rebuild his home. A woman told me she'd charged $50,000 of rebuilding costs to her credit card -- it was the only way she could pay for it.

Joe showed us his pool. It looked a lot like Diane's. He said he had snakes in his pool too. When he came home the first time, he found five feet of marsh grass all the way down his driveway, and his truck was half in the air up against his house at the far end of the driveway. He had to hire someone with a tractor to clear all the marsh grass just to get to his truck. Then he found seven snakes in his garage.

He explained how it happened. When the MRGO breached, the water rushed through a local marsh, then into a neighborhood canal. But the canal was much too small to hold the surge of water back. The small canal breached as well, and snakes from the marsh poured into the nearby homes.

We talked with Joe for a while. He even said it would be OK to videotape the waterline on the inside of his home. It was many feet above the top of the front door. Seeing it gave us a visual reminder that a person in a one-story home would have had to dive down and swim underwater just to get to the door.

When it was time for us to go we walked across the street toward our car. I was looking around at all the destruction when I realized I was about to step on something. I looked down to see what was there -- a dead snake. I'm glad it was dead.

Back home in California, a few weeks later, I needed a ladder to change a light bulb. I went outside where we keep the ladder, but a big Daddy Long Legs spider had made a home between the rungs. "Eeewwww, forget it," I thought. I started to walk away but then I remembered Joe. I thought, "If he can deal with seven snakes in his garage, then I can certainly deal with one little spider." So I did.

From that point forward, St. Bernardians became my inspiration for courage and diligence. When I was faced with a challenge, I reminded myself that they had already dealt with colossal challenges beyond anything in my life. In St. Bernard Parish I learned that people do rise up beyond all expectations. They had experienced a catastrophe, yet they still managed to demonstrate a calm resolve and a belief that they would overcome the hardship. They didn't become consumed by misery, but they weren't in denial either. They grieved, cried, accepted the situation, and then got to work on starting over.

CHAPTER SIX

The House That Floated Down the Street

Before meeting Joe, I took Sandy to see where the brick house had somehow moved from its property and landed in the front yard of another home. It had smashed against the front of a white two-story home. We tried to figure out where the brick house had come from because there wasn't a house missing across the street or next door.

As we looked at it we noticed a teenage girl standing across the street. We asked if she was from the area and she said, "Yes, that's my house," as she pointed to the white house with the brick house in its front yard. I asked what her family thought when they first came back and saw it. She answered, "We…" But her voice cracked. She hesitated, looked down, put her hand over her heart and was silent as she composed herself. When she looked up I could see she'd fought back the tears, and she finished her sentence even though her voice was still cracking, "We cried a lot." I don't think I'll ever forget that girl. She had to be so strong at such a young age.

She pointed down the street and said if we kept driving about halfway down the block, we'd see the lot where the brick house had once been. It had floated that whole distance. She said her family planned to rebuild when the brick house was removed. We gave her a Home Depot gift card and asked that she give it to her parents. She thanked us, and then asked if we might have a wire coat hanger. She'd come to the neighborhood with her boyfriend to see the house, but he had accidentally locked his keys in the car. Now they were stranded in this empty neighborhood with no one to help. We didn't have a coat hanger, but got out of our car anyway to help them scrounge for one in the piles of debris.

The debris piles were about four feet tall all the way down the street, so we had a lot of material to work with. We spent about half an hour with them, finding all kinds of potential tools to open the car and giving each one a try. We could see the car keys sitting on the driver's seat. Some tools worked better than others -- a broken golf club worked the best. But even when we were able to make contact with the unlock button, it failed. It was exasperating. The boy used his cell phone to call a family member for help, but no one was able to come.

The wind was howling and there were all kinds of eerie sounds as it blew through the skeletons of houses and caused open doors to bang against walls or slam shut. The girl looked around, then hugged herself and said, "It's creepy out here." Sandy and I had been thinking the same thing, but this was unfamiliar territory for us. To hear the comment from someone who'd lived there made it feel even creepier.

After a long time struggling with the lock, the boy became resigned to the idea of smashing the car window to get inside. But it was his mother's car, so we all knew that had to be the last resort. I'd remembered seeing a man with a pickup truck around the corner and back a few blocks. I told them I'd try to find him to see if he had any good tools we could use.

I felt some sense of urgency because the two of them had planned on seeing the Parish parade that day, and they were missing it because of the mishap with the car. The girl kept saying, "I can't believe we're going to miss the whole parade." Sandy and I had already seen how uplifting the parade was for the people of The Parish, and I wanted this couple to have some of that happiness too. They'd been through enough disappointment already. So I ran around the block and down the street, hoping we could get the car opened before the parade was over. When I got there, the pickup truck was gone. But I saw something even more promising, a couple of trucks and a group of five or six men standing nearby.

As I approached, I noticed they were all wearing matching polo shirts embroidered with the name of a local construction company. The men turned to me as I approached, but they didn't smile. They looked guarded. I knew they were being cautious because there were rumors of outsiders coming to The Parish to loot homes.

One man asked, "Can we help you, ma'am?" I told them what we were doing and asked if they had any tools we could borrow. They looked a little skeptical. One joked that maybe we should just break a window. When I explained that the car belonged to the boy's mother he said, "Oh, then don't break a window, his mamma will really be mad at him."

Then another asked, "Where y'all from?" The minute I said the word California I saw the guarded expression on his face melt and he blurted, "Thank God for y'all! You don't know how much it means to us that you come all the way here to help us." He immediately pulled out his cell phone and said, "I'm going to get you some help." He called a friend from the sheriff's department, but the friend was working the parade and couldn't leave. I thanked him for trying and ran back to Sandy and the teenage couple.

On my way back I noticed a small white pickup truck with its front end on the ground, and the back end in the air, leaning against a fence. The sight of it didn't shock me as much as the realization that I'd passed it at least three times before I really noticed it. In any other place it would have attracted the attention of everyone within miles. But scenes like that were so common in The Parish, after a while you didn't really see them anymore.

As soon as I saw Sandy and the couple they started jumping up and down shouting, "We did it! We did it!" We gave them quick hugs and told them to hurry in the hopes they'd catch at least the end of the parade.

Then Sandy and I looked for the lot where the brick house had been built. We found the lot across the street and eight houses down from where the brick house landed. It had floated for half a block. If I hadn't seen it for myself, I never would have believed it was possible.

CHAPTER SEVEN

This Is Home

After helping the teenagers and meeting Joe, Sandy and I went to look for the oil spill zone. I had a vague idea of the streets that had been affected. But it was easier to find than we expected because we discovered an ominous sign posted on the side of the road with a skull and crossbones and the words, "Poisoned by Murphy Oil Company."

We turned down a nearby street and saw a group of people standing in front of a FEMA trailer. A slim pretty woman in the group looked at us and smiled. We rolled down our window and asked, "Is this the oil spill zone?"

She smiled again and said it was. She walked over to our car to continue the conversation. She told us more about the effects of the oil on the houses. Sandy told her, "We feel so bad for you guys."

But she looked almost insulted. She replied, "Oh, don't feel sorry for us. We're rebuilding our home, we have a trailer to live in, and we still have jobs." She felt lucky because some people in The Parish had lost family members. She told us her name was Molly. She didn't have the attitude you might expect from someone whose home had been destroyed by floodwater and crude oil. She was one of the happiest, most grateful people I'd ever met. And we couldn't help but like her right away.

Within a couple minutes she told us to park our car and come in to see her house. As we walked up her driveway she said, "Y'all must be thirsty. You want a beer? Or some water?" And we gratefully accepted.

Her husband Buck had already gutted the house, cleaned it, and replaced the electrical wiring. It was stripped down to the frame and they hadn't put up sheetrock or flooring yet, but they'd already put a sofa and a TV in the living room. She pointed to the room and said cheerfully, "This is where we watch American Idol." She proudly showed us her new refrigerator in the kitchen, which was also gutted to the frame. She pointed at the wood framed walls and joked, "Well, I always did say I wanted an open floor plan."

Buck and Molly's two dogs followed us around on the tour of the home. You've heard people say pets often resemble their owners. Well their smaller dog, Fifi, was just like Molly. I've never seen a smiling dog before, but I swear this dog really did look like she was smiling. I commented on how happy Fifi looked and Molly said, "She is happy, she just got a new collar today."

Buck was equally welcoming and happy. He teased us for talking like Californians and told us we needed to start saying "y'all" instead of "you guys." He told us about his love for The Parish and all the great fishing spots nearby. He talked about his frustration with people in other parts of the country who didn't understand why anyone would move back there. He explained that he'd lived there all his life, and his friends and family lived there too. He said, "Where else am I gonna go? This is home."

I told him, "I understand completely, I want to live here too." It was ridiculous, but it was true. If you saw The Parish and heard someone say those words you'd think they had to be blind. Six months prior the entire Parish had been underwater. But if you took time to get to know the people, you'd understand. The people made The Parish a great place, not the buildings. I think they must have had strength and determination before Katrina, but I know they had it after. I wanted to live among them and learn from them.

Buck offered us some freshly boiled crawfish from an ice chest and showed us how to eat them. "You twist the head off like this..."

I told Molly I was surprised that people kept inviting me into their homes. I asked if they just wanted someone to see how their houses had been affected. But she looked a little puzzled, as if she didn't understand why I thought it was so unusual for people to invite strangers into their homes. She answered, "We're just like that here."

Molly introduced us to some of their neighbors who'd come back to The Parish for the parade. At that point in time, Buck and Molly were one of only two families on the block who'd moved back. Everyone else had moved away while they restored their homes and tried to decide what to do next. While we women chatted, Buck grabbed a big broom and swept the street. Molly explained that Buck had a Type A personality and liked to stay busy. He was doing his best to keep the neighborhood tidy.

All their neighbors were kind and welcoming. Their next-door neighbor, who they called "Buck Two," offered us a huge platter of sausage and ribs he'd just barbequed. They told us about the parade. It was an annual celebration, held the weekend before St. Patrick's Day. It was called the Irish-

Italian-Islenos parade, to celebrate The Parish's cultural heritage. People riding the floats threw beads, trinkets, potatoes, cabbages, carrots and onions to the crowd. If you thought about it, you'd realize the vegetables were all necessary for a good corned beef and cabbage stew. Buck Two showed us the trunk of his car, filled with items he'd caught from the parade. He handed each of us a shopping bag and said, "Go ahead, take anything you want from the trunk." When we hesitated, he grabbed large handfuls of beads and placed them in the bags. One of my favorites was a strand of green beads with an alligator hanging from it. When I went home I hung that strand of beads on my rearview mirror, as a reminder of the inspiring people I met that day.

As we visited in that neighborhood something occurred to me -- we hadn't done anything for these people, but they were doing everything they could to welcome us and feed us. I'd already run out of Home Depot gift cards by the time we met.

We told them we were coming back for Jazzfest the following month, so Molly gave each of us her business card and said, "Call us when you come back and we'll go party at Jazzfest together. And if you can't find a place to stay, come stay with us. We'll get some air mattresses for you." We were overwhelmed by her hospitality. She was living in a trailer in the oil spill zone while repairing her damaged home, but she was still offering to let us stay with her.

We took pictures of Molly and Buck and their neighbors. And as we were leaving, Molly hugged us. Buck was still sweeping the street, but he stopped and waved enthusiastically and shouted, "Bye, Californians!" We laughed as we drove away, commenting on how they'd made us feel like royalty. We didn't realize it at the time, but we'd just met people who would become some of our very best friends.

We corresponded by e-mail with Molly afterward and made plans to meet for Jazzfest. She sent messages about life in The Parish as the recovery continued. She shared her excitement over the re-opening of Walgreen's a few weeks after our visit. Her comments made me appreciate all the conveniences I take for granted every day.

CHAPTER EIGHT

Nothing But Love

We came home just before St. Patrick's Day. I composed a St. Patrick's Day e-mail for my friends, describing the parade and the inspiring people I'd met. On a whim, I decided to send it to four people from The Parish. I was nervous about how they'd react to a visitor's perspective on their hometown. Their response caught me by surprise. Within a few days I received dozens of e-mails from Parish residents who'd received my e-mail as it was forwarded from person to person. Each message carried the same theme -- thank you for seeing the good in our Parish, we love it too.

Date: March 17, 2006
From: J Young
Subject: St. Patrick's In St. Bernard
To: My Friends

Happy St. Patrick's Day! Last weekend I witnessed the most joyful St. Patrick's experience, I have to share it.

I was in St. Bernard Parish, Louisiana -- one of the most devastated areas in the state. You've seen the Lower 9th Ward on TV -- well St. Bernard Parish is right next to it, and every single person there lost his home in the flood.

But here's the amazing thing. Last Sunday they celebrated their annual St. Patrick's Parade. It's a big deal there. I went there with my sister and her friend to do some volunteer work, but everyone we met asked, "Did you come for the parade?"

On Sunday we drove down the main street in The Parish, on our way to visit some neighborhoods to see what we could do to help. But it turned out that we were driving down the parade route right before the parade started. There were hundreds (possibly thousands) of people lined up 3 people thick on the sides of the road waiting for the parade. They were laughing and smiling, most wearing green of course. They looked so happy you almost didn't notice all the collapsed buildings right behind them. But when you did notice, it was the most surreal scene you could ever imagine. Joy in the presence of devastation. In that moment they were so happy to be reunited and have their parade that they were oblivious to the horrendous scene that stretched for miles in all directions around them.

Just a few miles away, in New Orleans, the people throw beads to the crowd during Mardi Gras. In the St. Bernard Parish St. Patrick's Parade they throw beads too. They also throw carrots, potatoes and cabbage! All the main ingredients for a good corned beef and cabbage stew, minus the corned beef, which I imagine would present a huge health hazard if it were thrown! It's an annual tradition, and these resilient people weren't going to let anything (not even hell or high water) get in the way of an annual tradition.

We were still out in the neighborhoods talking with a few people who stayed behind to gut their houses when the parade ended. The people who'd been to the parade came home to their trailers parked in front of their flood-damaged homes with trunks full of beads and vegetables. They all had huge smiles.

They told us to take whatever we wanted from their trunks. They offered us food they'd barbequed for the celebration.

Here we'd come to help them, and they were doing everything they could to help us. One woman gave us her phone number and told us to come stay with her family the next time we were in the area. Everyone hugged us and welcomed us and thanked us for being there. And these words kept popping into my head -- nothing but love. Everything else was gone, but the love was still there.

I told some of the women I was amazed at how resilient they all were. One of them said this was an especially good day because of the parade. "But believe me, we still have our days of crying, too."

If you drive through St. Bernard Parish you understand the crying part. I saw things I never thought I'd see. A brick house, still attached to its foundation, that popped out of the ground and floated past 8 houses until it crashed into another one. And I met a sweet teenage girl who lived in the house it crashed into. When I asked her about her house, her voice cracked and she fought back tears. But when I asked her about the parade she beamed.

People around the country keep asking why those affected by Katrina don't just move away. And in St. Bernard they say, "Because this is where my people are." And now I understand what they mean. They reminded me of the Whos in Whoville who celebrated even when the Grinch took everything away. Katrina hadn't stopped St. Patrick's from coming. It came! "Somehow or other, it came just the same."

So if you're walking around today and someone pelts you with a potato or a cabbage, don't be offended. It's probably someone from St. Bernard Parish just sharing the love.

I hadn't anticipated that my e-mail would be forwarded to so many people, or that they'd be so grateful for it. Many of them referred to St. Bernard as "The Forgotten Parish," and thanked me for bringing attention to it.

One woman told me her house was almost completely rebuilt. She invited me to come to her home for a fresh seafood dinner the next time I was in The Parish. She even said I could bring my friends. I couldn't believe someone I'd never met would invite me over for dinner.

Even as the two-year anniversary of Katrina arrived, I was still receiving occasional e-mail from Parish people, thanking me for writing about them and their parade. The one that choked me up the most came from a Marine. He wrote:

> "I came back from Iraq a month after Katrina to see the devastation to my hometown and my family and friends' homes. I appreciate seeing people like you volunteering and getting out the word of what really happened to the little spoken about St. Bernard. You guys are heroes to me; I only got to spend a month back home to stay and help out my family and friends. I just want you to know we appreciate you and thank you!"

The other comment made by many of those who wrote was a request, "Please keep telling the rest of the country about us. We still need a lot of help."

CHAPTER NINE

What Matters and What Doesn't

Sandy and I went to St. Bernard Parish for the third time at the end of April 2006, eight months after Katrina. We had made reservations for this trip before Katrina was ever on the radar. It was going to be our annual Sister Bonding weekend. We'd planned on going to Jazzfest, because locals had told us it was the best entertainment New Orleans had to offer. But after Katrina hit, we and many other people wondered if Jazzfest would be possible at all.

We had just been in The Parish six weeks prior to our return for Jazzfest. Sandy and I talked excitedly about going back again so soon. We were looking forward to the celebration of Jazzfest, but I couldn't help feeling it would be a wasted trip if I didn't get out to The Parish and do something to help.

So I packed my steel toe boots again and my relief worker shirt, breathing masks, leather gloves and grubby jeans. I had about 50 packets of flower seeds that I'd planned on leaving at the relief center the last time and forgotten. Sandy and I thought it might be worthwhile to plant some flowers there, because so much of the vegetation had been killed off in the flood. We wanted to bring a little color and life to The Parish to lift the residents' spirits. So I packed a tiny shovel and a little claw tool for weeding. And we both tried to keep our minds open about what we'd do when we got there.

We went to Jazzfest on Saturday and had a great time. It took place at a fairground in New Orleans, with multiple bands playing simultaneously on different stages. The music was terrific, but I enjoyed the food booths the most. We stood in line for just a few minutes, and walked away with steaming hot bowls of jambalaya.

We saw the Mardi Gras Indians perform, which was a real treat because we'd heard so much about them. Then we sat on the grass, among the crowd at the big stage, and listened to the Dave Matthews Band. It was a privilege to be in that crowd for the first post-Katrina Jazzfest. We were among the faithful, who hadn't given up on the city. We kept meeting people from Northern California. Some of them said they'd been coming to Jazzfest for years, and they weren't going to let Katrina stop them now. A group of friends from Florida sat next to us on the grass. One said he had worked for a contractor, clearing debris in the early weeks after Katrina. He said the smell was something he'd never forget. "It was so bad, I kept vomiting in my mouth." He was astonished that the city had found a way to make Jazzfest happen.

The next day Bruce Springsteen was scheduled to perform in the evening at The Fest. We wanted to see him, but we felt a strong pull to get out to The Parish too. We wanted to do some work and see Molly and Buck again. Molly had signed up to volunteer at a benefit, so she couldn't go to The Fest. So we planned to work in The Parish, stop by their house, then try to make it back to New Orleans in time to see Springsteen in the evening.

We got out to The Parish in the late morning, after working through the logistics of finding some food and securing a rental car. And once we were there, nothing else really mattered. We never did make it back to hear Springsteen, but we didn't mind. Being in The Parish put everything in perspective.

We stopped first at the new site of the relief center, in the parking lot of the Adullam Christian Fellowship Center. There we met Pastor Randy in person for the first time. We'd spoken to him by phone and e-mail several times. And we'd worked at the relief center he coordinated on two previous occasions. But until this point, we'd never actually met him. The relief center was closed this day due to a lack of volunteers. Pastor Randy said he felt badly because people kept driving up and then driving away when they saw the center wasn't open. When I got home from this trip I saw Anderson Cooper on TV with over 3,000 volunteers just a few blocks away in the Lower 9th Ward. But this relief center didn't have any.

We told Pastor Randy we'd brought flower seeds and thought we'd do some planting. He said we should get in touch with his friend Mark, who'd been coordinating volunteers to plant flowers to help welcome people back to The Parish. Pastor Randy asked a nearby friend, "Do you have Mark's number?" Within a couple minutes we were talking to Mark on the friend's cell phone. Mark told us it'd be great if we could plant some flowers at "the gates to The Parish." This would be on the center divide (or as they call it, "the neutral ground") of St. Bernard Highway near Jackson Barracks.

When we got off the phone, Pastor Randy and his friend informed us that Mark was one of The Parish councilmen. Since we had Mark's blessing, we shouldn't have any problem if someone questioned us about digging up the neutral ground. The friend told us he'd known Mark since they were kids, and that Mark was a man of integrity. We'd heard rumors of corrupt government officials and didn't know if they were true or not. But the friend assured us that Mark was a good man dedicated to helping The Parish residents.

While we were still at the closed relief center, I had a few minutes to talk with a woman who was a member of Pastor Randy's church. She and I talked while her son played nearby. She told me Pastor Randy had coordinated volunteers to gut and rebuild homes. They'd worked on her home, and her family was so excited because the work was almost completed. They'd been living in a temporary home outside The Parish while their house was being repaired. She told me the volunteers didn't want her to have to work on the house. So one day she was sitting in the backyard while they were working and she was overcome by a feeling of bliss, even though the house was so damaged, because she was home. And she said, "I knew without a doubt that there's nowhere else in the world where I'd rather be."

After a while, the woman and her family left, and so did Pastor Randy. Sandy ran across the street to a newly opened dollar store. I stood there alone as I waited for Sandy to return. Before long, a man drove up and said he'd come to get some water, but the center was closed. No one else was around to help, so we searched together until we found the water and he took a gallon bottle. I asked if he needed more, but he assured me one bottle would be enough. A few minutes later an elderly lady approached and said she'd come for water and bleach. So we found the items together and she too assured me that one bottle of each would be just fine. She went back to her car and returned a few minutes later, carrying two armloads of toiletries and other high-demand items. She said, "I brought these to donate." It surprised me to see someone repaying the relief center. She didn't want to take without giving something back.

Sandy and I went out to the spot Mark had told us about and started digging. Within a couple minutes a sheriff's car approached and we were glad we could tell him that Mark had given us his blessing. After we had been working for about 20 minutes, a vehicle approached with "Mark Madary, Parish Councilman" painted on the door. A friendly man hopped out and coaxed a little boy out of the passenger seat. Mark held out two bottles of drinking water for us. He introduced us to his nephew, who looked to be about four years old. He told us he was raising the little boy now. "We lost his mamma after Katrina." The little boy was cute and playful. Mark told us the boy had been out to the same spot on previous occasions, helping his uncle plant flowers. They couldn't stay long, but talked with us for about 10 minutes before they had to leave. Mark had been in The Parish when Katrina hit -- government employees were required to stay. He described what it was like to be stranded on a rooftop, then pointed down a nearby street and told us about rescues that had taken place there.

One thing we learned quickly in St. Bernard Parish was that every person there had an interesting story. And I don't mean a story as in a fabrication, but a story to share about the effects Katrina and the flood had imposed on each individual's life. Many of the stories were heartbreaking, but most of them were inspiring. Because no matter how bad things were, people still had hope. Many admitted to feeling depressed, but all had at least a glimmer of faith that things would turn out all right. When we asked people how they'd been affected, just about everyone responded with, "We lost everything." But they didn't say it with a tone of self-pity. They'd say it matter-of-factly, as if they were telling us about the weather, "Well, it's going to be warm today." "Well, we lost everything."

I've heard it said that everything's relative. And I guess when everyone else you know lost everything, your loss seems less tragic in some ways and more tragic in others. Some people would add, "but we had flood insurance, so we'll be all right," or "but we only had six feet of water, so we can rebuild." They'd say, "Some people around here got hit really bad." And when you'd point out that the person speaking had been hit pretty hard too, they'd say something like, "Yeah, but we got through it OK, some other people lost family." One man, whose house and neighborhood were completely wiped out, said, "Have you seen Plaquemines Parish? Those poor people need some help."

As Sandy and I continued to work on the neutral ground, cars whizzed by at about 50 mph. There were quite a few people who waved, honked or yelled, "Thank you!" as they passed. One man pulled over and shouted out his address. He laughed and said, "When you get done here, I can use some help at home." I asked if he really needed help, but he said he was just joking around. He asked where we were from, and when I told him, he said he'd met several other volunteers from our home state. He told me not many residents had come back to The Parish. "We used to have about 65,000 people here, and now only about 10,000 are back. It's hard because there's no one around to talk to."

It was still surprising to hear people open up and share their feelings with a complete stranger in just a matter of minutes after meeting. But in the environment they lived in, there was no use for small talk. The complete destruction of multiple cities gave the residents a clear distinction between what matters in life and what doesn't. They didn't have any need for things that don't. And I think that's one of the qualities I loved about them the most.

I've never been one to throw the word love around lightly. Even in my romantic relationships, I've never been the one to say the word first. Love has always been something I hold too much respect for to proclaim it without sincerity and certainty.

But I frequently heard and said the word there. And it was spoken with complete honesty. "We love y'all." "We love you guys." And more often than not, the words accompanied big bear hugs. It was a brotherly love that had nothing to do with romance, and everything to do with the soul.

Clearly Katrina was a life-changing experience for the people of The Parish. And to a lesser but still significant extent, it changed those of us who experienced what Katrina had done to them. As volunteers we were privileged to witness their strength through the toughest of times. Most of us wonder what would happen if one day we lost everything. But we don't spend much time pondering it because it's just too ugly and frightening to think about. But when I went to St. Bernard Parish that question and the answer were in my face. I couldn't escape them, that's all there was for miles.

I think they loved us for caring, and we loved them for demonstrating that people can hold on to their best qualities even when they're living through their worst nightmare. We often hear that people will behave like animals when they're reduced to survival mode. One might expect a dog-eat-dog mentality to reign in such an environment. But there was no evidence of that here. In St. Bernard Parish dignity and compassion, humor and hospitality were still going strong.

And if these residents could maintain their goodness in these circumstances, maybe we could too if disaster ever visited us.

CHAPTER TEN

Every Day Is A Good Day

Even with all the destruction, there was still something beautiful about The Parish. Being there felt a lot like being in church, because I was surrounded by believers. Everyone who moved back to The Parish had faith. For many it was faith in God. But for others it might have been faith that things would get better. Maybe they just believed in their own ability to rebuild their cities. But everyone believed. There was so much faith you could almost feel it in the air.

If you didn't have faith, you couldn't stay there. If all you could see was the destruction, you'd lose your mind. You had to be able to see a future beyond the current situation to keep plugging away, day after day, through all the inconveniences and all the loss.

It sounds strange, but I felt the presence of God there more strongly than almost anywhere else. Every turn I took and every encounter seemed divinely guided. I always met the most inspiring people and learned the most powerful lessons. It was as if The Parish and the people amplified my awareness of a spiritual presence.

I saw an online video of Habitat for Humanity volunteers gutting houses there. They were all grinning from ear to ear. When I saw it, it brought back memories of how gratifying it always felt to be there. At the end of her stay, one of the volunteers said, "I'm taking my soul back with me." Her words were perfect and poetic and her sentiments felt so familiar.

We saw dozens of Virgin Mary statues on front lawns when we drove through The Parish. I'd never seen so many of those statues in one place. The house behind her might have been utterly destroyed but Mary was still standing, in all her glory. And once again, there was something perfect about that. Mary is the ultimate symbol of acceptance. When the angel told her what her future held she didn't run and hide. She accepted it and trusted that everything would turn out for the best.

I talked with a woman who demonstrated that absolute faith. She told me about her first trip back to The Parish after the flood. When she and her husband saw their devastated home and community she said, "We have a choice." He told her they didn't -- the choice had been made for them. She said, "No, we have a choice. We can believe that God has a plan for us or we can roll over and die, and I'm not ready to do that yet."

There was no lack of faith at the Adullam Christian Fellowship Center on St. Bernard Highway either. In late April, eight months after Katrina, most of The Parish was still in disrepair, most residents still displaced or living in FEMA trailers. The church was still being rebuilt, the new sheetrock up in only about half the building. But people had taken pens and written bible verses and messages of inspiration on the sheetrock: "God Is Good All The Time," "Every Day is a Good Day," "Love Life," "God is the Rock."

If I were a resident I don't know if I'd have that much faith. I hope I would, but it might be too hard. But that's what made the people there so inspiring. They proved to me that it's possible.

Some people told them they were fools -- that they should cut their losses and run. Only time will tell if they made the best choice. For now, it's anybody's guess. Back in the 70s the scientists said earthquakes in California would eventually cause it to break off and fall into the ocean. Today even the scientists laugh at those old warnings. Who knows if today's dire predictions for South Louisiana will be viewed the same way in the future?

But in the meantime, when I want to know what deep faith looks like, I go to St. Bernard Parish. It's not so difficult to be a believer when all is right with the world. It's when your world turns upside down that you find out what's really at the core of your soul.

So I keep rooting for the people who've returned to The Parish. I want to see their towns come back strong because I want their faith to be rewarded. And maybe all of us will witness a resurrection there.

CHAPTER ELEVEN

I Know You

Sandy and I finished planting flowers on the neutral ground and decided to drive through neighborhoods to give out more Home Depot gift cards. We went to the oil spill area and found ourselves in a neighborhood that surrounded St. Mark's Catholic Church. But the neighborhood was deserted for block after block. Residents weren't sure it was safe to live in a place that had been polluted by crude oil. The only signs of life were the weeds that had overtaken the brown and shriveled lawns.

We saw an ADT Security Systems van standing upright, with the tail end leaning against a home's roof and the front end on the ground. It was disheartening to see that even the businesses hadn't found a way to recover their property eight months after the flood.

We drove a little further and spotted a man, woman and teenager in front of a house. The man approached when he saw our car, so we offered him a gift card. He refused it at first, saying he didn't need it. But by the looks of his neighborhood, it sure couldn't hurt for him to take it. So we insisted, telling him he could give it to someone else if he didn't use it.

He said he was rebuilding because he wanted to see The Parish recover. "But then sometimes I come out here and look around and I have to ask, am I just kidding myself?" He looked exhausted. For a minute he leaned his arm on the roof of our car and rested his head on it. Then he pointed to his neighbors' houses and described each family's situation. "That family's not coming back, that family isn't either. This family is still trying to decide."

I knew he had to drive past that ADT van every time he came back to work on his house. And I imagined that must be demoralizing for him. I had hope that maybe it would bring him some encouragement to see the van removed, to see some kind of progress in the neighborhood.

I'm an ADT customer, so I e-mailed a photo of the van to their customer relations department with a request that they remove the van. ADT responded within one day, thanking me for bringing it to their attention. They said they'd just hired a new manager for the local office in the previous two weeks. They promised to have the van removed within a week. But I never heard anything from them again, even though I sent e-mail inquiries. So I was left wondering if they ever did the work.

When I returned to The Parish, three months later, I took a drive through the neighborhood to see if the van was gone. But it was easy to become disoriented because the flood had washed away the street signs, and I wasn't sure I was on the right road. Houses that had been landmarks for me had been torn down. I saw a man in front of a house, so I stopped to talk to him.

He told me he was working on his mother-in-law's yard. The Parish government was requiring people to keep their yards maintained, in an effort to revitalize the community for those who were trying to come back. It sounded silly in some respects, and brilliant in others. Because it's difficult to maintain the yard of a home you had to abandon, but it's also hard to have hope for your city when it's being swallowed up by weeds. The man said Murphy Oil Company had cleaned the oil from his mother-in-law's home, and he thought they'd done a pretty good job.

I asked him about the ADT van. I was pretty sure it had been on the same street as his mother-in-law's house. He wasn't sure, but a few minutes later his wife drove up and gave the answer I'd hoped for, "Oh, yes, the ADT van is gone."

I blurted out a "wooohooo!" and started clapping. And with some embarrassment, I realized I must look like a complete Bozo -- any kind of positive news in The Parish made me cheer. But I wanted to send a thank you letter to the people at ADT for doing the right thing. And I hoped other businesses would follow their lead.

But my story of the residents on that street doesn't end there. Fast forward to January 2007, six months later. My sister Sandy brought her husband to The Parish so he could see it for himself. And she wanted him to meet Buck and Molly.

One night they made plans to meet Buck and Molly for dinner in New Orleans. Molly told Sandy they'd invited a couple of friends to join them. As they waited in the restaurant lobby, a couple walked in. The man looked at Sandy and said, "I know you. You drove through my neighborhood in St. Bernard Parish with another woman and you gave me a Home Depot gift card." It was the same man who lived down the street from the ADT van and had wondered if he was kidding himself about rebuilding. His name was Johnny, and it turned out he was one of Buck's best friends. And, in fact, he and his fiancée were the friends who'd be joining them for dinner. But when Buck and Molly made the dinner arrangements, they didn't know Sandy had already met Johnny in the oil spill zone nine months earlier. Sandy was amazed that he remembered her face after such a brief meeting and the length of time that had passed since.

Two months later, I traveled back to The Parish with Sandy to do some volunteer work with The St. Bernard Project and to see the annual Irish-Italian-Islenos parade. It was the same parade we'd passed a year earlier. We were invited to a big party at Buck and Molly's house after the parade. Many of Molly's relatives were invited to the party and I was excited to meet them. Their friend Johnny was invited too, and I wondered if I'd recognize him.

But I didn't. He looked different. I think maybe because he looked so much happier than before. He'd decided not to move back to the house in the oil spill zone. He had purchased a nice house in another neighborhood that had been flooded by "only" eight feet of water. I asked him and some of the others if they were writing down their memories of what had happened, so that future generations would understand. He told me he was too busy rebuilding to write everything down. He laughed and said, "How about if I just tell you, and you write it for me?"

After talking for a while at the party, he said he wanted to show me his new house. So six of us piled into his SUV and he drove us there. It was still in the process of being rebuilt, but it was a beautiful home. And it was good to see positive things happening for him after all he'd been through.

On the way there he said he wanted to tell us something about the day we met him in front of his house in the oil spill zone. And I remembered that day again. We'd rolled down our car window when we saw him and asked if he was rebuilding. He approached the car, while his fiancée and another family member stayed close to the house.

On the ride to his new house he said, "I have to tell you something about that day. When you left, you had us all in tears. We couldn't believe people would come all that way to help us out." Johnny was paying us a compliment, but at the same time, it saddened me that they had no expectation of receiving help from other Americans.

At the time, it felt like such a small gesture to give a $25 gift card to someone whose entire house was destroyed. But Johnny's gratitude was similar to what we'd found in a lot of Parish residents. The smallest token of help was appreciated so deeply because it meant a lot to know that anybody cared -- or even knew about them.

Two years after Katrina, I spoke with him again. He said he would never forget the volunteers who'd come to his parish.

He added, "If a big disaster ever happens again, anywhere in the US, I'm going there to help." And I believe he will.

Then, two and a half years after Katrina, it was Johnny who invited us to watch the Mardi Gras parades from that incredible viewing stand. It had benches, a speaker system, a DJ and even a porta potty. We had all the conveniences any parade-watcher could want. The stand was an expensive luxury -- so Johnny and his family had split the cost with nine other families. It was large enough to accommodate close to 100 people, so there was plenty of room. But Johnny's invitation was just one more example of how Parish residents often responded to a small kindness -- they repaid it with a more generous one.

CHAPTER TWELVE

Katrina Funk

I wanted to gut a house so badly. It was like an itch I needed to scratch. Ever since my first visit to The Parish, I'd been trying to find a way to make it happen. But Habitat for Humanity required volunteers to stay for a full week. And I couldn't stay that long. I thought about just driving through neighborhoods until I found someone working on a house, and then offering to help. But I didn't know if anyone would accept.

Sandy and I went to The Parish in July 2006, just before the one-year anniversary of Katrina. And we had house gutting at the top of our list of things to do. We weren't sure how, we just knew we'd find a way. When Molly heard, she told us to pick her up on the way to wherever we were going -- she wanted to help out too. Never mind the fact that she was still living in a FEMA trailer and rebuilding her own house. We asked Molly if she wanted help rebuilding her home, but she declined. As always, she was determined to put other people ahead of herself.

Molly greeted us with hugs when we picked her up in front of her FEMA trailer. She told us about the latest challenges and successes in the area. We asked her about her daily life as the recovery continued. Molly worked in New Orleans and most people there understood how severely St. Bernard had been damaged. When they heard where Molly was from they often said, "Oh, I'm so sorry." But Molly told them, "Well please don't be sorry, I'm not. I love my parish."

Pity was not appreciated by most of St. Bernard's residents. Concern was appreciated, compassion too -- but not pity. They were proud of their community, no matter what Katrina had done to it. Pity was just plain insulting.

The three of us got reacquainted, then hopped in the car to look for someone to help. As we drove and talked, Molly said her daughter's boyfriend, Sal, had just purchased his first home. It was a house in Arabi that had flooded to the rooftop. An elderly woman had lived there before Katrina, but didn't want to come back. So she sold her home to Sal. He was young and willing to work hard to rebuild it. Sandy and I smiled at each other and asked, "Um, has he gutted the house yet?" Molly knew what we were thinking, but she insisted we should help someone less fortunate. Sandy and I argued that everyone who was rebuilding could use some help. Sal had worked alongside Molly as she'd gutted her own home, so she liked the idea of returning the favor. And we liked the idea of helping someone who'd helped her. So after a little persuading, she phoned Sal and made the arrangements.

We headed to his new house and met him there with Molly's daughter Erin. The house was in the same neighborhood where Sandy and I had seen The Trophy House on our first visit. It was the first neighborhood we'd walked through in The Parish. So it made us happy to have this opportunity to work on one of those homes. It was still early, a good thing because the morning held the promise that this would be one hot and humid July day. Sandy and I brought our own bottled water, facemasks, safety goggles, steel toe boots and gloves. Erin and Sal brought the shovels and a wheelbarrow.

Sandy and I were the only ones who wore the safety goggles and facemasks. I knew we looked like uptight rookies. I hardly ever saw the locals wearing this garb. It was a little embarrassing to wear it while I worked beside residents who'd done this before and didn't use much protective gear. But I'd promised my husband I would. If I hadn't made that promise, I probably wouldn't have worn them. Peer pressure. But I was grateful for that tetanus shot I had before I came, and I was rethinking my decision not to get a hepatitis booster.

Sal and his friends had removed the flood-damaged furniture a few days earlier. So we cleaned out the kitchen cabinets and tackled the foot-high pile of debris that covered the floor. It turned out to be a lot easier than I expected. House gutting is pretty simple once you accept that it's going to be a little yucky.

We started on the debris that covered the floor. A lot of the items on the floor had become stuck to each other as the floodwater dried. We had big but lightweight shovels that worked perfectly. We scooped debris into the wheelbarrow and took turns emptying it on the sidewalk. The debris pile was full of destroyed clothes, books, linens, decorations and utensils. A man in a truck stopped and foraged through the pile for copper. A little while later, another man came for the same purpose. People were selling copper from destroyed homes to help make ends meet. Inside the house, the level of debris was slowly going down. When we reached the bottom we had to use a little extra elbow grease, because the debris was stuck to the floor.

We moved on to the kitchen, where the warped cabinets were barely clinging to the walls. We opened them and roaches ran out. The dishes, pots and pans still had 11-month-old floodwater in them -- it was smelly and brown. We carefully removed them, trying hard not to splash the water in our faces or on the person working beside us. I no longer regretted my goggles and facemask.

We worked for several hours and completely gutted all but two rooms. I guess it would have taken longer if the woman who'd previously owned the house had been there. She might have wanted to sift through it all to look for anything worth saving. But she wasn't there. So it was easier to do the job, because we didn't have to be mindful of possessions that may have held emotional value.

But there were some items we discovered that left a lasting impression on me. One of them was an 11-month-old petrified banana. And I found a Christmas potholder that looked just like one I had at home. It made me stop and wonder what my possessions would look like if they'd swirled around in the Katrina Punch and then been left to ferment for almost a year. What hit me hardest was a photo album with "Our Wedding" on the cover, and then page after page of runny colored lines that didn't look like they'd ever been part of a photograph. I thought about keeping that ruined photo album. I don't know why, maybe because it had been important to someone once. It felt wrong dumping it in the pile on the sidewalk.

Molly and I stood in one of the bedrooms. We looked up and saw the light fixture on the overhead fan was half-full of water.

It looked like a fish bowl. I remembered seeing a man at the relief center, back in December, wearing a soaking wet shirt. He said he'd been removing a light fixture in his house when it broke and floodwater poured out of it onto his head, chest and shoulders. He'd come to the relief center to ask for just one shirt from the pile of donated clothes, to replace his drenched t-shirt. And he asked for one bottle of water, which his wife helped pour over his head, face and chest to clean away the nasty floodwater. I'd had a hard time imagining how that could have happened. But now, looking at the overhead fan in Sal's house, I understood completely.

There was an odor in that house -- and all the other flooded homes -- that I'd never smelled before. Some residents called it "Katrina Funk." It was something like the odor you'd create if you combined mud, wet hay, hot overripe peaches, dirty toilet water and the musty moldy smell of the Pirates of the Caribbean ride at Disneyland. The only way to get rid of the smell was to remove everything but the frame of the house. It was the kind of stench you never forget, and it covered our shoes and clothes. I threw away my work boots when we were done because I didn't want to bring the smell home with me.

We were all covered in sweat -- our hair was dripping, our clothes were saturated. But it wasn't as miserable as I'd expected. I was accustomed to sweating like crazy on hot days in karate class. But I'd seen photos of volunteers working in big plastic body suits -- they must have been working in January. In the heat of July, a plastic body suit might as well be a body bag -- you wouldn't last five minutes in it. We wore shorts and tank tops. And if a little bit of stinky sludge got on our arms or legs, we didn't worry about it too much. But when we were done, Molly, Sandy and I used up an entire container of Wet Wipes to clean our arms and legs. And later that night, after Sandy and I took showers in our room, the dirt from our bodies left a black greasy film in the tub below.

My favorite part of the day was taking down the sheetrock. We used a sledgehammer and a crow bar. I liked the crow bar best. You'd slam it into the sheetrock, then pull, and a big chunk of water-damaged wall would snap out and fall to the floor. It didn't take much effort at all. We joked about how it could be a great way to relieve stress.

I'd decided on that trip to take extensive video of The Parish and try to make it into a comprehensive story of what was happening there a year after Katrina. I wanted to film the gutting process, but didn't want to do it for long, because I wanted to stay focused on the work. I brought the video camera in for a minute and everyone continued talking and joking as we had been throughout the gutting process. Later, when I edited the video, I had to mute the sound because the sound of laughter didn't mesh with the scene of a destroyed house. I knew it would look insensitive. But the truth is, it would have been insensitive to mope around while three people whose homes had been destroyed found a way to stay cheerful as they gutted yet another home. And there were residents all over The Parish doing the same thing -- staying positive, holding on to hope and laughing even when they were standing in a pile of Katrina Funk.

When I think back on days I've worked in The Parish, that day stands out for me as the most rewarding. It felt good to get my hands dirty and do something that might make even a small tangible dent in the recovery process.

CHAPTER THIRTEEN

Y'all From Here?

We finished gutting Sal's house in the afternoon. Molly called Buck on her cell phone, then told us he was planning a shrimp dinner for all of us. In the meantime, we drove through The Parish while Molly explained what had happened in the different neighborhoods.

She told us about the shrimp boat that had floated into a neighborhood. I remembered hearing about it from Mr. Williams, the first person I met when I went driving around by myself in March. I was surprised to hear the boat was still there eleven months after the flood. Molly said she'd take us out to see it. When we arrived, I pulled out my video camera because I knew it was something I should include in the video story of The Parish. Sure enough, a big boat was blocking the entire street, with one end of it in someone's front yard. The boat had to have floated across at least two miles of the city to arrive in this neighborhood. Next to it were the remains of two houses that had been flattened into piles of rubble.

Sandy and Molly walked ahead as I filmed, and I noticed two men behind me walking toward the boat. We exchanged hellos, and one asked, "Y'all from here?" We talked for a while and they agreed to let me question them on film about the effects of the flood. They were a father and grown son from the city of Violet, another section of The Parish. The father said he and all but one of his grown children had lost their homes. He added, "It's tough to start over." He told me they'd moved across Lake Pontchartrain to Slidell, something many St. Bernard residents had done after their homes were destroyed.

Both of them told me the whole Parish had been devastated by floodwater from the Mississippi River Gulf Outlet (MRGO). They spoke of their uncertainty about coming back to The Parish until the MRGO was closed. Otherwise they'd face the possibility of another flood in the future.

Parish residents and officials called it "The Mister-Go," and they'd been trying to get it closed for years. It was a federal project, built by the Army Corp of Engineers 40 years earlier with substandard materials. The Mister-Go was built through marshland that had been a natural hurricane buffer. And it brought saltwater from The Gulf into that freshwater marshland. Before long, the vegetation in the marsh was killed by the saltwater intrusion. And the natural hurricane buffer was gone. In addition to that problem, the levees of the MRGO eroded and sank, making the walls shorter and less durable than they needed to be for adequate protection. The residents had questioned what would happen if a large hurricane blew through. They nicknamed the channel "The Hurricane Highway" -- which proved to be prophetic.

Hurricane Katrina pushed a tidal surge into the MRGO, creating a wall of water higher than the levee walls. The water spilled over the earthen levees, which caused them to dissolve quickly and collapse. The mass of water that flowed into The Parish was so large, it effectively turned the 500 square mile Parish into a lake. And that lake was over 20 feet deep in some sections.

We'd seen signs around The Parish with the words, "MRGO Has Got To Go." After Katrina, the Army Corp of Engineers finally conceded that the canal should be closed, and recommended that Congress approve the closure. Now it was just a matter of getting Congress' approval and waiting for the work to be completed. The best-case-scenario projections estimated the completion of the closure would take several years and several hurricane seasons.

The two men at the shrimp boat chatted with me for a while. The father said he was lucky because he'd purchased flood insurance, even though he'd been told he didn't need it. The son pointed to a small canal behind us and said it had breached in about a hundred different places when it was overtaken by water from the MRGO. I could see it was important to them for people outside The Parish to understand their situation. They'd seen the national news reports and couldn't help noticing that their story wasn't being told.

As they prepared to leave, we heard the surprising sound of an ice cream truck. We couldn't believe it. We looked around and saw it -- on the same street that was blocked by the boat -- just about half a block away. Sandy commented on the contrast of the destruction with the merriment of the ice cream truck's song. We ran to the truck, not just because we wanted ice cream, but also because we wanted to meet the driver. He turned out to be a man probably in his 40s with a thick accent I didn't recognize. He was grinning from ear to ear. He spoke with the enthusiasm of a child. "I've been here in St. Bernard Parish for four months," he said. "Same route, same schedule every day."

I noticed the menu posted on his window included lunch items. I guessed his truck was probably the only source of meals for a lot of the volunteers and families who were gutting homes. We complimented him on his willingness to bring this service to an area that badly needed it. We bought ice cream from him, and after a long hot day of gutting, that ice cream hit the spot.

We got back in the car and Molly took us through different neighborhoods in different stages of repair. Some still looked devastated and some showed signs of renewal. One Chalmette neighborhood was full of enthusiastic residents who had restored their homes so beautifully -- it almost looked as if nothing bad had ever happened there. Many of the homes even had flowerbeds full of colorful blooms. It was encouraging to see what they had accomplished. But not far away, another neighborhood was in upheaval. Molly told us about the homes that had been on Delambert Street. We drove there, and even today it's still shocking when I remember what we saw. I could only hope that no living person was in that vicinity when the hurricane and flood tore through, because I couldn't imagine how they would have survived.

The homes were of newer construction, pretty one-story homes with nice accents and details. They looked like homes my friends live in. But they weren't on the same street where they'd been built. They'd floated off their street, across a small canal and into a neighborhood on the other side. Most of them had landed in the middle of the road. Many had crashed into other houses. Trucks and cars were buried underneath the homes. We could see pieces of the cars poking out from underneath. One house had crashed into a stop sign and an apartment building. Between the homes, there was a huge pile of debris that stretched for about half the length of a football field. In the pile were cars, chairs, clothes, bikes and who knows what else.

Just outside one of the houses were other cars at lopsided angles, with doors and trunks wide open. I hoped that didn't mean people had been in those cars, trying to escape when the water raged into The Parish. Residents who'd stayed through the storm said the water went from floor to ceiling in less than fifteen minutes -- not enough time to jump in their cars and drive to dry land anywhere. And, as at many other places in The Parish, there were things here that tugged at my heart. I saw a flooded Barbie ride-in Jeep abandoned in the dirt near one house -- it looked just like one my daughters had at home. Most alarming to me of all was a baby swing, smashed up against the inside window of one of the houses that had floated away.

I grabbed my camera and started filming again, because people had to know about this. How come no one knew? I'd heard so many awful stories about the Lower 9th Ward, but that was just one neighborhood in one city. What about all the other neighborhoods and all the other affected cities? In New Orleans alone, the neighborhoods of Lakeview, Gentilly and

New Orleans East were decimated. St. Bernard and Plaquemines Parishes were completely wiped out. And then there were all those coastal towns in Mississippi, too. While volunteers and donations were streaming into the 9th Ward, the other areas were often neglected because the country wasn't aware of how badly they needed help. So I shot video of the neighborhood, hoping I could raise some awareness about even one of these devastated communities.

We left that neighborhood still shaking our heads in disbelief. We drove to Molly's house where Buck greeted us with smiles and hugs. He asked if we'd ever been to a shrimp boil. Uh, no, what the heck was a shrimp boil? Just what it sounded like, he explained.

Buck had a giant pot attached to a propane tank in the middle of the driveway. It was simmering with spices, corn, potatoes and celery and it smelled like a little piece of heaven. He was aided by his friends, Dennis and Buck Two. Buck Two and some of the other neighbors we'd met in March were there to welcome us again. Buck made sure we watched as they poured fresh shrimp into the pot. He grabbed my video camera and filmed it. He told us we had to show it to our families back in California.

When it was time to eat, none of them were fazed one bit by the fact that there wasn't a functional kitchen or dining room in the house anymore. They grabbed a picnic table and took it inside, placing it in the middle of the gutted kitchen with its wood-frame walls and concrete floor. They laid newspaper over the entire table. Then Buck grabbed my video camera again and directed his two friends to bring in the shrimp. They brought the pot to one end of the table, tipped it over and poured the shrimp out over the entire length of it. The steam rose and the smell of Cajun spices filled the air. We gorged ourselves on piles of fresh seafood and vegetables. It's not that we'd never had shrimp before. But in California we'd pay $20 for a plate of ten big shrimp. Our Louisiana friends were shocked when we told them -- it was one more thing that made them grateful to live where they did. We went back to our room that night with bellies full of beer and shrimp. But before we left, Buck told us to make sure we brought our families back with us the next time, so they could have some good Louisiana shrimp too.

As we drove back to our room in The Quarter, we noticed the locally owned businesses in St. Bernard were slowly reopening. Most of the large chain stores and restaurants were still closed. But those that were owned by local residents were making a comeback. Business owners from St. Bernard understood that they were a vital part of the recovery process.

The next day I drove through The Parish alone, meeting people and hearing their stories. I felt driven to do this, and I wasn't exactly sure why. But it was similar to the pull I'd felt to go to The Parish just after Katrina. It was just something I needed to do. I wanted to meet people and try to understand their predicament. And the more I talked with people there, the more it seemed that many of them really wanted to talk. I think they were still sorting out what had happened, and talking about it helped them to process it. People seemed almost grateful to be asked how they were doing. It occurred to me that they probably didn't talk about their losses with each other much, since everyone they knew was struggling with their own losses. Sharing sad stories would only bring them down. But someone from outside the area could listen.

As I drove, I saw an elderly woman sitting in the front yard of her flood-damaged home. I stopped to talk with her and she greeted me with a smile. She had a cheerful demeanor, laughing and making jokes. She'd been in The Parish when the flood poured in. Her grown children had helped her, making sure she got to safety. After they'd evacuated, she heard reports of how badly the flooding had spread. She said, "I thought we'd been wiped off the map. But here was my house, waiting for me." She was delighted that some trees had survived the flood and were blooming. Her children were working on her home periodically, while they also worked on their own homes. She was living with one of her sons until the repairs were completed.

She proudly showed me the mailbox in her front yard. Most mailboxes had been knocked down in the flood and storm. Mail delivery had been suspended, so residents had to line up at the post office to receive their mail. But The Parish government had recently announced that mail delivery would begin when a total of 500 mailboxes were restored. In a community where there had been 27,000 homes before Katrina, there were still less than 500 standing mailboxes almost a full year after Katrina. So this woman was proud of her mailbox, not only because it would benefit her, but also because it was part of an effort that would help everyone in The Parish. She showed me the flowers she'd planted around the mailbox, saying she'd done it to greet the mailman.

I drove through another neighborhood where half the homes were missing and the rest were badly damaged. I noticed most of them had the letters "KEN" spray painted near the front doors, and I wondered what that marking meant. I saw a woman wearing work gloves standing near her home. She and I were the only two people around, so she stopped and looked up as I drove toward her. I introduced myself and within minutes she invited me into her house to see the work that had been completed. She'd done a lot of it herself. The house had been gutted, stripped and cleaned down to the frame. It was easy to see this woman was smart and diligent -- someone you'd want on your team if the you-know-what ever hit the fan.

A car pulled up and her two young children hopped out of the back seat. They stood beside us as we continued talking. I asked the woman what the "KEN" marking meant. Without batting an eyelash she explained, "The name of the body recovery team was Kenyon International. So they painted 'KEN' on each house after it was searched." This group wasn't one that searched for survivors. They were the ones responsible for claiming people who had died and transporting them to the morgue. Standing there and looking at this young family, it made me shudder to think someone had searched for dead bodies in their home. And, since the children were there, I didn't want to ask if anyone had been found.

We heard a loud rumble, the sound of a thunderstorm approaching. The children looked nervous and asked their mother if they could leave. They wanted to go somewhere that felt safer, and so did I. So I thanked the family for inviting me in, and drove back to The Quarter where the storm had already passed.

A few days after our trip, Molly was standing in her yard when she heard the familiar sound of an ice cream truck as it drove down her street. It was the same truck we'd seen near the shrimp boat. The ice cream man recognized her. He leaned out the window and asked, "Hey, where are your friends?"

A few weeks later there was more news about the shrimp boat that floated into the neighborhood. Someone had intentionally set it on fire. There'd been some dispute about who was responsible for removing it. Apparently, someone was tired of waiting for a resolution, so they took matters into their own hands. The boat still had so much fuel in it that it burned for 12 hours. But the firefighters saved what was left of the flood-damaged house beside it.

Back at home, I spent all my spare time editing the video I'd shot in The Parish in my effort to tell St. Bernard's story. I stayed up until 3:00 am some nights working on that video. But it was a labor of love. If I could've worked on it without sleeping at all I would have. When it was finished it was 31 minutes long. It was too long for YouTube. So I gave it the title "Beyond New Orleans - St Bernard Parish One Year After Katrina" and uploaded it to Google Videos.

Within days I received e-mail from about a dozen residents, asking how they could buy a copy of the video. I told them I'd send it for free. The most surprising e-mail came from a woman who complimented my work and said her home was in the video. After some e-mailing back and forth I learned something that gave me a chill up my spine. She had lived in one of the houses from Delambert Street that floated across the canal -- the house with the baby swing smashed up against the window. Fortunately, the family had evacuated before the flood. She told me the homes had recently been demolished.

"All of the homes were demolished this past weekend. It's so strange. It's hard to put in words our feelings. It's like our lives, or should I say, the life we knew never existed...We just keep telling ourselves, by this time next year things have to be better...You just get used to seeing the house every time you pass, and then...all of a sudden it's gone."

She hadn't asked for a copy of the video, but I offered to send her one. She said she'd love a copy since they didn't have any videos of their home. The flood had destroyed their camcorder.

Almost a full year later I logged on to Google Videos to check the status of the video I'd made. It'd been viewed over 3,500 times. In the comments section a young man had posted this message:

"In the beginning of this video, my house is shown. There's that house that floated slab and all across the street. My house was the house with the white truck on the fence. I lived in St. Bernard all my life. I didn't move back; we decided it was just too unhealthy. I'm amazed my house made this video…It's just so sad... it's crazy how my house made this. Thanks for making this. It's nice to see home once and awhile."

I realized both of these residents appreciated having video of their homes -- even though the video showed those homes destroyed -- because it was the only way to see them at all. It led me to a new appreciation for my own house, and made me wonder how I'd feel if it only existed in videos or photographs.

Relief Center in Wal-Mart Parking Lot – December 2005.
Residents lined up on left, relief workers are on the right.

Sandy, on far right, preparing items for distribution.

This house in Arabi had a refrigerator and child's picnic table on the roof. Debris and flooded cars covered the front yard.

The same house a few months later with a Marine Corps flag. Shortly after this photo was taken, this house was demolished.

Military Police kept us safe in The Quarter.

Storefront in Chalmette with sign demanding closure of the MRGO.

Brick house that popped out of the ground and floated down the street, landing in a family's front yard.

One of many Virgin Mary statues in The Parish. Someone decided this one needed help and gave her a walker.

Kudos to ADT for removing this van.

Sandy, Molly, Me, Erin, Sal and his dog after gutting Sal's house.

Inside Sal's house, Me and Sandy hold pieces of sheetrock while Sal and Erin take down more sheetrock behind us.

Molly took us to see this shrimp boat still blocking a street eleven months after Katrina.

The cheerful ice cream man brought food and music to this devastated neighborhood close to the shrimp boat.

This house from Delambert street floated across a canal and into another neighborhood, where it landed on top of a truck and next to a brick apartment building.

After house gutting, Molly, Sandy and I relax…

…while Buck prepares a shrimp boil dinner.

This home was flooded and struck by a tornado. With typical Parish humor, the owners posted a sign in the front window that read, "Come In, We're Open."

Sandy and Molly at the Irish-Italian-Islenos Parade, 2007.

Gabrielle and Claire with an abandoned dog at The St. Bernard Parish Animal Shelter. The dog later found a home in Canada.

Jim and Buck pour shrimp onto a table while Charlie watches.

Claire holds a bag of stuffed animals she brought to Adullam Christian Fellowship Center for distribution.

Molly and Gabrielle bring in a crab net at Bayou LaLoutre while Cathy, Buddy, Buck and Katey watch.

Claire holds a blue crab at Bayou LaLoutre.

Molly, Sandy and I watch the Mardi Gras parades in 2008.

CHAPTER FOURTEEN

Anticipation

Buck had told us to bring our families back with us, but he didn't have to work hard to convince me. I'd wanted to bring my family for a long time. But I'd hesitated because I was concerned it might traumatize my children. The one-year anniversary of Katrina had passed and The Parish was still in recovery mode, but it looked much better than it had in the early months. The flooded cars had been removed, most of the debris had been carried away, and the houses that had floated off their foundations were completely gone. I talked it over with Jim and we decided to go as a family.

I was so excited. I loved New Orleans and couldn't wait to share it. I loved The Parish too, and knew my family would understand my obsession with it when they saw it for themselves. I scribbled a few thoughts in my journal shortly before our trip:

I'm going back to New Orleans one week from today. I found my <u>New Orleans for Dummies</u> book (1st edition -- the best one) and when I opened it I found my fold out map of New Orleans. Just seeing it made me give a little shout, "Yesss!" And seeing the names of the districts and the streets makes my heart beat a little faster -- St. Philip St., Royal, Decatur and, of course, Bourbon.

Jim tells me I'm obsessed. Every time I see a fleur de lis, or anything pertaining to New Orleans, I stop and take notice. There are only two other places in the world that make me smile like this -- the town where I lived as a kid and Rome, because how can you not be awed by Rome?

But there's a difference in the way New Orleans makes me feel. In many ways it feels like home. It feels like a place where people get me and I get them. New Orleanians respect silliness and revelry. It's not just something that's tolerated or permitted, like in other parts of the country. It's part of the culture. Some who don't know the city well think of it as a southern Las Vegas -- all decadence and debauchery. And if you go to New Orleans looking for those things, you can surely find them. But if you go there looking for your soul, you will find it there too.

Each time my plane lands there I am filled with an overwhelming desire to step out and kiss the ground. The first time back after Katrina I thought, "This time I'm really going to do it." The problem is that the first place you step into is the airport. After seeing all those horrific images of dying people lying in the airport in the first days after Katrina, the idea of kissing the floor is too disturbing. I have thought maybe I'll just kiss The Quarter when I get there. But anyone who knows what happens in The Quarter on Friday and Saturday nights knows that's not such a great idea either. So I'll probably just have to settle for hugging The Quarter. No one there will really mind or even pay much attention -- they're accustomed to absurd behavior and they don't judge it.

On a post-Katrina trip, in the first Spring since the storm, I noticed how all the passengers in my plane were laughing and smiling as the plane landed and taxied. Many seemed downright giddy. I said to Sandy, "Only in New Orleans does everyone look this happy when the plane lands." A local overheard and said, "Las Vegas. People are smiling this much when their planes land in Las Vegas. The difference is they aren't smiling on their way home." When I told Jim about this he said, "People are happy when they land in any vacation destination." I told him, "Yeah, but in New Orleans the locals are smiling too." Especially after Katrina, because after almost losing it, they realized just how much they loved their city.

This will be the first trip to New Orleans for the girls and Jim, and I wonder what they'll think of the place. I don't know if they'll love it like I do. The feeling is kind of like the one you get the first time you bring your boyfriend home to meet your parents. You love him and you want them to love him too. But if they don't, it's not going to change the way you feel about him.

Here are the things I'm looking forward to sharing with them: the Mississippi River, the food (Oh my Lawd, the food!), the New Orleans accent, Zydeco music, the French Market, Café du Monde, the architecture and -- most of all -- the spirit of the people.

And here are the things I want to do: #1, absolutely, without a doubt, is go to St. Bernard Parish and do something to help people who are trying to rebuild. And maybe videotape a little, to help spread the word about their situation. Then, for fun, go to Swampfest, ride a boat on the Mississippi, eat chocolate fondue at the Melting Pot, eat at Café du Monde, and walk around Jackson Square. And food we definitely have to have: jambalaya, muffulettas and beignets.

CHAPTER FIFTEEN

The Other Side of the World

I wanted my family to enjoy this trip and I wanted them to help in some way too. But it was a challenge to find a non-profit group that would allow young children to volunteer. At the time, Gabrielle was ten and Claire was seven. One of my frustrations with the larger relief groups was that they seemed to be bogged down by red tape and liability concerns. I needed to find a group that would allow my children to participate in the recovery process. So I went to an online forum for the New Orleans area and asked if anyone had suggestions. Someone wrote back, saying the animal shelter in St. Bernard Parish was in grave need of volunteers. At times there was only one person to run the entire shelter, which was still overrun with Katrina strays.

This looked like it might be the answer. My daughters are devoted to animals. They'd love nothing more than to run their own dog and cat sanctuary. I knew it would be a perfect fit for them, but was concerned the shelter wouldn't want children helping. I called the shelter director to ask. She answered, "Bring whoever you have, we need the help."

Personally, I wanted to help people with their homes more than anything. But I knew my interests had to take a back seat on this trip. I'd already had trips to indulge my own needs to help. It was my family's turn now, and I had to let them do work that would be most meaningful to them. I would have more opportunities in the future. Jim wanted to work on homes, so I called Molly to ask if she or her family or friends could use an extra pair of hands. She said she'd ask around.

The trip to New Orleans was an eventful one. On the morning of our flight, at about 2:00 am, I woke to the sound of Jim throwing up in the bathroom. Apparently he had food poisoning from the fast food we'd eaten for dinner. By 4:00 am it was clear he wasn't in any shape to fly. We decided that I'd take the girls to New Orleans and Jim would catch up with us in a day or two. But, as I drove to the airport, my phone rang. It was Jim, saying he was coming after all -- he'd meet us at the airport. But as we were boarding the plane, Jim said, "I'm not going to make it. I love you guys, have a good trip," and he ran for the bathroom. The three of us were concerned for Jim and sad that he wouldn't be coming with us. We settled in for the long flight. Then, just before take-off, Gabrielle shouted, "Look, there's Dad!" Jim had thrown up in the airport bathroom and then returned to board the plane. By some stroke of fate or luck he was seated beside a doctor. Jim slept for most of the flight, and was sick only once in the airplane bathroom.

He was feeling much better by the time our connecting flight landed in New Orleans. Jim was immediately taken with the architecture of the French Quarter. And the whole family was pleased with the accommodations and the friendly staff at the Lafitte Guest House on Bourbon Street. After a while we went out to The Parish. Jim drove while I directed -- pointing out the Wal-Mart parking lot where the relief center had been, the first neighborhood I'd walked through, and the house we'd gutted in Arabi. My family was mostly quiet, taking it all in, trying to absorb it.

We found the animal shelter and were told they were just about to close for the afternoon. Most of the work had been completed for the day. So we told them we'd come back the next day to help.

We met Leanne, a volunteer at the shelter. I asked how she was doing since Katrina. She said she'd been in The Parish when Katrina brought the flood. When I asked more about it, she got that far-away look in her eyes that so many Katrina survivors get.

She was from Poydras, one of the communities of The Parish that was closer to The Gulf. Many of its residents were commercial fishermen. She stayed during Katrina because her elderly father refused to leave. Over time I encountered a lot of middle-age adults who stayed because their parents wouldn't leave. Many elderly people had lived through Hurricane Betsy, and they thought it could never get worse than that. If they made it through Betsy, they reasoned, they could certainly make it through Katrina. But sadly, some of them didn't.

Leanne said the water came up so fast that she and her father barely had time to get in their boat. She said they floated around for days before they were rescued. Unlike in New Orleans, there wasn't an area of dry ground where they could take refuge. By the time they were rescued and taken to a shelter, they had been wearing the same clothes for seven days. She shook her head at the memory of it.

But the rest of her story was much worse. Her brother drowned in the flood. As she told me about it her eyes welled up and she fought back tears. "But he saved four people before he drowned," she said. It was clear it brought her some comfort to know that. Instinctively, I moved to hug her. And all I could say was, "I'm so so sorry," over and over. But they felt like such small useless words for such a big loss. How do you make it better for someone who's been through that?

She told me she'd had her brother's dog in her care when the flood hit. She kept him with her in the boat. But days later, when help finally arrived, she was told the dog could not come with them. She was forced to make a choice between saving her father and saving the dog. She left the dog on what remained of a levee, promising herself she'd find him within a day or so. She didn't know the residents wouldn't be allowed back in The Parish for a month after the storm. When she got back to The Parish she searched for the dog, but never found him. I didn't ask, but I suspected that had something to do with her volunteer work at the shelter. Maybe she hoped the dog would turn up there someday.

We went back to the animal shelter the next day to help. It was heartbreaking. The cats were housed in cages on the floor that were about six feet tall. Each cage had from four to ten cats in it. We watched as a volunteer hosed down the concrete floor to clean the waste. To stay dry, the young cats leaped up to platforms in their cages that were about three feet above the ground. But the older cats, who'd lived through the flood, became panic stricken. They climbed the cage walls till they reached the top and clung there with their paws wrapped around the cage wires. They hung from the tops of the cages, wailing and crying.

Most of the dogs were in cages on concrete with no bed and nothing soft or warm to lie on. It was mid-November, and that concrete floor was cold. One of the dogs had a limp hind leg that just hung and she hobbled on the other three. She had gashes all over her body, each about two inches long. She looked like maybe a Lab mix. She was really friendly and had these haunting eyes that just stared at us as if she were pleading for help. Leanne told me the dog had been hit by a car. With conditions in the shelter as poor as they were, I didn't know if that dog would ever make it out.

We noticed the dogs were cooped up in cages and asked if we could walk them. Jim took care of the big dogs, and I took the smaller ones. Gabrielle and Claire helped as well. Some of the puppies were so excited to get out of their cages and run that they wet themselves. With such a shortage of staff, we doubted they were walked as frequently as they would've liked. Other dogs walked slowly and followed my lead. I could tell a few of them had been leash trained in their life before the shelter. I fell in love with a little Dachshund. She shook like a leaf until I took her out of her cage and held her -- that seemed to soothe her. Leanne told me she'd been shaking since she first came to the shelter. And she'd been there for two weeks. It pained me to think about that little sweetie shaking all the time.

The harsh reality was that most people in The Parish were still living in trailers as they tried to rebuild their homes. Many of the fences in the yards had been knocked over in the storm and flood. Most people in The Parish didn't have a place to keep a dog, especially a large one. The only hope for most of the animals was to be adopted outside The Parish. And I had to believe people all over the country would help if they just understood the problem. I asked the director if she'd like me to take video of the dogs and cats and post it online. She told me, why not? It couldn't hurt. So I took video of all the animals.

We noticed the shelter was lacking in some essential supplies, so we went to find a store. The new Winn Dixie had finally opened just after the one-year anniversary of Katrina. It was the first large supermarket to open since the flood. There was no doubt that the re-opening was significant to the community. The Parish president, council members, the school board president and the superintendent of schools all attended the Grand Opening. The store was big and beautiful -- beautiful because of the sheer fact that it was there at all. I looked around at all the people inside -- women with their children, adults helping their elderly parents, store clerks with smiles on their faces. Everyone looked so *normal*. You'd never guess they'd all been personally affected by the tragedy of Katrina.

I was amazed by their resilience. I wanted my children to learn from their example. I leaned down and whispered to Gabrielle, "Look around at all these people, every one of them lost their home."

The look on her face was skeptical. "How do you know?" she asked.

"Because everyone who lives here did."

I knew it was a lot for her to take in. It was a lot for me to take in. Right there in the Winn-Dixie we were seeing proof that life goes on, no matter how bad things get. People still find a way to pull themselves together and move on with their daily tasks.

I'd spoken to Molly earlier in the day, and she'd invited us to come over when we finished at the shelter. So we took our purchases to the animal shelter, then made the short drive to Buck and Molly's home. They welcomed Jim and the girls with as much enthusiasm as they'd welcomed Sandy and me the first time. My family instantly liked them and loved doting on their two dogs. Buck and Jim got to know each other and decided to go to Buck's friend's house. His friend was rebuilding and needed some help installing insulation. This would be Jim's opportunity to help someone rebuild, and he was anxious to get started.

After visiting for a while, the girls and I decided to go back to The Quarter and get our souvenir shopping done while Jim was working. Molly told us to come back for a shrimp boil in the evening. We drove through the Lexington neighborhood before leaving The Parish. I tried to take some video of the progress there, and the lack of progress. But the devastated neighborhood was too frightening for the girls. They were afraid to get out of the car. But to my eyes, the neighborhood looked so much better than it had in the early months after the flood. So I stood by the car as I filmed, and if I stepped more than a few feet away from it, my youngest would call for me. I still have the video with her frightened voice in the background, "Mom, where are you going? Mom, come back."

I decided it was best to forgo the filming this time. I got back in the car and drove. Around the corner, we spotted a few people walking in the otherwise deserted neighborhood. I stopped and asked if they were rebuilding. They told me they were from Colorado, but they were moving to The Parish to help rebuild. They were interested in buying one of these houses, to repair it and live in it. "The people here are so great," they said. We exchanged stories of the warm and welcoming people we'd met.

We drove back to The Quarter and went to the Gazebo Café for a late lunch. I had jambalaya, Gabrielle dove into some red beans and rice and Claire gobbled up half a muffuletta sandwich. We enjoyed the music of a live jazz band that played nearby. While we were eating, a woman at the next table looked over at Claire and commented on her big muffuletta sandwich. She asked where we were from and when I said California, she said she had family there. About 20 minutes later the woman came over to our table to talk a bit more. She told us she was from Algiers and always came across the river on Saturdays to enjoy the city.

When the woman left Gabrielle asked, "Mom, why do you talk to strangers so much here?" I answered, "Because people here are so friendly." Being around them made me friendly too. But I noticed the opposite was true for me at home. While I was more outgoing in Louisiana, I was becoming more introverted in my own town. After I'd met so many people in Louisiana who were grateful for the smallest blessings, I started noticing that many of my conversations at home were about trivial concerns. We had it so easy, but we still managed to get stressed out about small things like dentist appointments or house cleaning. I wanted to be friendly with people at home, but I was losing my ability to make small talk. I couldn't think of anything to say. The only thing I wanted to talk about was St. Bernard Parish.

In the evening we went back to Buck and Molly's house. They wanted to make sure Jim and the girls got to experience a Louisiana shrimp boil like I had on my previous trip. We ate and laughed and talked until way past the girls' bedtime. When it was time to go, Buck and Molly gave us a care package of food to take with us, in case we got hungry later. Buck said he hoped this was just the beginning of a long friendship between our families. He joked that it was nice to have friends "from the other side of the world."

We drove back to our room in The Quarter and made plans for the next day. I'd wanted my family to help with the recovery process, but I also wanted Jim and the kids to enjoy the unique entertainment that New Orleans had to offer. I didn't want them to remember it as a place of only destruction. I wanted them to understand what it was before Katrina, and what it would be again. So we designated our third day of the trip as a play day.

We took the ferry across the Mississippi River to tour Mardi Gras World in Algiers. This is the place where the big Mardi Gras floats are built and stored. The building and floats had been subjected to some of Katrina's wind damage, but had been spared from flooding. Before the tour, we were shown a brief film about the history of Mardi Gras. I'd never been to Mardi Gras before, but that film sure made it look like a lot of fun.

We explored the warehouse and took turns dressing up in Mardi Gras costumes and taking pictures.

When we were done, we took the ferry across the river and headed out to the Audubon Zoo, where Swampfest was in full swing. Swampfest is held at the zoo annually to showcase local Cajun and Zydeco musicians. The lineup included one of my favorite Zydeco singers, Rosie Ledet. I had some of her music on my iPod, and the girls and I would often sing to it at home. My favorite Zydeco band was also performing at Swampfest, Rockin' Dopsie Jr. and the Zydeco Twisters. The area just below the stage was filled with hundreds of people dancing to the music. And local food was offered at nearby booths.

Our favorite section of the zoo was the swamp habitat filled with alligators. In one exhibit a zoo employee sat at a table with a young alligator in his hands. One hand held a firm grasp on the lower body and another gripped the gator's closed mouth. Patrons approached to pet the small gator. We followed along and did the same. But as I was petting the alligator I realized this was probably not fun for him.

I asked, "Does it bother him when we touch him?"

The zoo employee looked unconcerned. He shrugged his shoulders nonchalantly and replied, "There's nothin' he can do about it."

On our way back to our room we stopped at The Melting Pot for a fondue dinner and, of course, some dessert. Sandy and I had discovered this restaurant shortly after Katrina at the recommendation of our guesthouse manager. He said the business had just opened, despite the fact that few residents had returned and there was a shortage of customers and employees. We admired the restaurant owners for taking that leap of faith.

The food was good and the staff was interesting. Our waitress on our first visit had been a concierge at a major hotel before Katrina closed it. Her apartment had flooded and she was sleeping on a friend's couch until she could find a place to live. On our second visit, our waiter was a young guy from South Carolina who'd moved to New Orleans post-Katrina, because he loved the city and wanted to participate in its revival. People like the employees and managers of The Melting Pot were largely responsible for bringing New Orleans back -- because someone had to stick it out through the tough times, to ensure there was a viable city for everyone else to come home to.

Gabrielle and Claire loved their first experience at a fondue restaurant. We ate until we were stuffed and headed back to our room. We all spread out on the big comfortable king-sized bed. I asked the girls what had been their favorite part of the trip up to that point. I thought they'd say Mardi Gras World or Swampfest. But they both agreed their favorite experiences had been working at the animal shelter and visiting with Buck and Molly. That was another big lesson for me. I'd wanted to entertain them to make them love the area. But they taught me that even children get the most enjoyment from connecting with others and helping out.

When I'd come home from my first trip to The Parish, a year earlier, my girls understood something big had happened there and wanted to help. Claire decided to do some fundraising of her own. She drew pictures, because drawing is one of her greatest talents. She begged me to help her set up a booth where she could sell her drawings to raise money. So we set up her old lemonade stand on a bike path near our house and displayed her drawings. We offered soft drinks for a dollar and drawings for three dollars. Traffic on the bike path was sparse and sporadic, but she managed to raise about $45 dollars. She wanted to use the money to buy toys for kids in St. Bernard Parish whose toys had been destroyed in the flood. We found cute stuffed animals and Beanie Babies and packed them in her suitcase.

We brought the toys to distribute on our last day in The Parish. Claire wanted to hand them out personally. So we went to the newly opened McDonald's to look for kids, but none were there. We quickly realized it was about 2:00 on a school day, so most of the kids were in class. Claire really wanted to give the toys away in person, but we needed to get back to The Quarter to pack for our trip home. We decided our best option was to take them to the relief center at the church. Jim and Gabrielle waited in the car while Claire and I went inside. We chatted with a local volunteer. Claire gave him her bag full of stuffed animals and we told him how she'd raised the money. He promised he'd give the toys to local kids who came to the relief center.

On our last night in the room, Claire stretched out on the bed and said, "When you guys go back I want you to leave me here, so I can live here forever." She knew there was no way we'd leave her behind, but said she still planned to live there someday. I told her I'd come along with her.

On our last morning we went to Café du Monde for beignets. A local musician named Hack Bartholomew stood on the sidewalk, singing and playing a trumpet. He was taking requests, so I asked him to play "Do You Know What It Means to Miss New Orleans." I knew he probably had requests for that song a hundred times per day and told him so. He said,

"More like 3000 times a day, but 3001 isn't gonna hurt me." As we left we noticed he was selling CDs of his music, so we bought one that included the songs "Down By the Riverside" and "This Little Light of Mine."

We took a quick walk through St. Louis Cathedral, and I bought a couple of things at the gift shop for Claire's upcoming First Reconciliation celebration. Then we walked to Central Grocery Store, which is famous for its muffuletta sandwiches. We ordered one big muffuletta to take on the plane for lunch. Dang, that muffuletta was good -- much better than any airline food.

About a month after our trip, I finally finished editing the video I'd taken at the animal shelter and posted it on YouTube. Within a week it had been viewed over 500 times. I was surprised and hopeful that it would help. After some time, I received an e-mail from a New Jersey woman who volunteered at the shelter occasionally. She told me an animal behaviorist from Canada had seen the video and had dedicated herself to finding homes for as many of the dogs as possible. A woman named Susan from Connecticut had volunteered to travel to the shelter and arrange transport for the dogs. As a result of their efforts, Canadian families adopted dozens of animals from the St. Bernard shelter. As the third anniversary of Katrina approached, these women were still volunteering to secure out-of-state and out-of-country adoptions for the dogs and cats from the St. Bernard Parish shelter. And the volunteer from Connecticut continued to post videos of the available animals on YouTube under the user name MissBoomer. It still blows my mind when I think about it. I'd hoped Americans would help when they saw the video and understood the need. But I never anticipated help would come from Canadians too.

But maybe I should have, because I remember so many countries offered to help in the early days after Katrina. What a beautiful testament that was to the goodness of mankind. So often we hear about discord between countries. But we received so many offers of support from countries all over the world. Countries we had considered enemies even offered to help. And as Americans seek to help those who suffer from tsunamis in Thailand, earthquakes in China or cyclones in Myanmar, we understand how compassion transcends borders.

As I reflected on this, I remembered something Molly mentioned while we were having dinner at her home. She and her sister Cathy had gone to the first Saints game in the Superdome after Katrina -- in the same place where so many people had waited for help after the storm. The residents of New Orleans and its suburbs packed the newly restored Dome to celebrate their team and their dedication to the city. The television cameras were there to capture the moment. And

Cathy held up a sign that read, "Thank you world, love NOLA."

CHAPTER SIXTEEN

Season of Giving

After our family trip, the kids were determined to help more. They talked about the animal shelter with their youth group at church. And the other kids were eager to pitch in, so they raised money for the shelter by organizing two bake sales.

Around that time, Gabrielle and Claire's school started advertising booth rentals for an upcoming craft fair. The girls asked if we could sell crafts to raise money for The Parish. We made Christmas ornaments and jewelry to sell. My favorite of the ornaments was a pig with wings. It was a reminder that miracles were possible. My friend Lynn made beautiful handcrafted earrings and donated them for our fundraiser. Some people bought our items strictly because they knew all the profits were for Katrina recovery. Our humble little booth raised about $400 for Habitat for Humanity's efforts in The Parish.

Gabrielle's 5th grade teacher, Mr. Miller, was fascinated with her trip to volunteer. His own wife had been actively volunteering with The Red Cross since the early days after Katrina. Mr. Miller asked Gabrielle all about her trip and spoke of it often to the class. At Christmastime he and his fellow 5th grade teacher, Mrs. Greenhagen, decided to have their students sponsor a single mother and her four daughters in The Parish. The children brought gift cards and presents to be mailed to Louisiana. And not long after, the mother and her daughters sent a thank you letter with the name of each student written in beautiful script.

All of this giving on the part of many people reminded me that people really do want to help. Sometimes they just weren't sure how to do it. If someone helped them find a way, they were glad to contribute.

Christmas neared and relatives asked what I'd like for a present. But the only thing I wanted was to go back to St. Bernard Parish. I honestly couldn't think of anything else I wanted more. One year earlier I'd had my first glimpse of Katrina's handiwork. And I'd come away with a huge lesson in the value of things versus the value of our experiences. Any joy I could get from a physical item would only pale in comparison to the happiness I felt when I was in The Parish.

I'd had glimpses of this lesson before -- when my father-in-law and later my mother-in-law passed away. I stood in their home among all their things and thought how unjust it was that their sofas and table decorations were still here even when they were not. It didn't seem right that their things could outlast them. I finally grasped the concept that when we die the only things we take with us are our experiences.

Seeing St. Bernard after the storm reminded me of the insignificance of our things. I saw the entire contents of people's homes lumped into a pile of decaying muck. In the following months, when I'd see some trinket in the store I liked, I'd ask myself, "If that item were laying in my flood-damaged house in a pile of muck would I dig through the debris to retrieve this item? Or would I leave it to be scooped up and dumped into a pile of garbage?" If my answer was that I'd leave it, I'd walk away without buying that item. Consequently, there weren't many things I wanted anymore.

The cost of repeatedly visiting Louisiana was adding up. Jim supported my trips, but didn't want to empty our savings account to pay for them. So I had to get creative about financing. I quit my karate lessons to save $65 per month. A black belt was no longer at the top of my priority list. I started digging through old change jars and jacket pockets and collecting everything I found in a bank the shape of a pig with wings. I'd read a book by Dr. Wayne Dyer in which he said we should give thanks for every penny we find. By doing so, we acknowledge the abundance in our lives. So I was grateful for every nickel and penny I found because it brought me a little closer to the $350 I needed to pay for a flight to Louisiana. I was astonished by how much money I found in my car, closet and laundry room -- old rolls of coins we'd had for 10 years or more and completely forgotten. When it came to purchasing things, I'd compare how much the items cost to the cost of a plane ticket. Someone would say an item was $500 and I'd say, "Five hundred dollars? That's more than a round-trip ticket to New Orleans!" It became the yardstick by which I measured all purchases.

So I told Jim and all my relatives that the one thing I'd most love to receive for Christmas was a gift card for American Airlines. They all listened, and I had one of the best Christmases ever -- opening those gifts and knowing I'd be going back to The Parish soon. By the time I added the gift cards to the money I'd scavenged from around the house, I had enough for a plane ticket. On Christmas day, at my parents' house, I looked at Sandy and asked, "How soon can you go back with me?"

Sandy and I chose to go back in March because we wanted to see the St. Patrick's parade again. By this time we'd learned the real name for it was the Irish-Italian-Islenos Parade. It was a celebration of the heritage of the earliest settlers in The Parish. Molly and Buck lived less than a block from the parade route and they invited us to watch the parade with them. They would be hosting a crawfish boil party for a big group of friends and relatives. The parade wouldn't be until Sunday, so we contacted a non-profit called the St. Bernard Project and volunteered to help rebuild a home on Saturday.

You may be wondering how I reconciled myself to leaving my family so frequently to take these trips. At first I felt some guilt over it. But I'm a mom who works at home. Even with these trips, I was still spending more time with my children than I would have been if I had a 9:00 to 5:00 office job. And I knew I was becoming a better mother and my children were learning important life lessons through this process. So I left the guilt behind and moved forward. And I started making plans to bring a very special gift to my family from New Orleans.

CHAPTER SEVENTEEN

Pets & Peeves

After working at the animal shelter with my family, I was convinced we needed to adopt a pet from the area. I tried to find out the status of the Dachshund and a Rat Terrier I'd seen in the St. Bernard shelter. But I was told they were both "gone." I couldn't bear to ask what that meant and decided to assume they'd been adopted.

After much thought, I decided a cat would probably blend best with our other pets. But I heard The Parish shelter was no longer taking cats. Rumor had it that the shelter cats had developed a nasty kitty cough, which proved to be fatal. So the choice had been made to stop taking cats, thoroughly clean the facilities and start again with a healthy environment.

I started searching on PetFinder.com for a cat from the area. I was interested in several cats, but one stood out from the bunch because of her story. She'd been born feral, as a result of

Katrina. And then, just a few weeks after she was born, a stray dog killed her mother. People in her neighborhood had seen her family for months, and had been leaving food out for them. But after a while they realized the cat family kept growing. They needed to be captured and neutered. A woman named Jane caught 15 of the strays and took them into her home. She had each cat vaccinated and fixed. When I heard this cat's story I wanted to help her. And when I saw her name I knew she was meant to be ours. Her name was NOLA, the name I'd already chosen for any cat we adopted, because it's the acronym for New Orleans, Louisiana.

I called Jane to make arrangements to meet Nola. She was a wonderful lady and we spent almost an hour on the phone together. She lived in Gretna, just across the river from downtown New Orleans. My plan was to meet Nola on my first day there, decide if we were a match, then pick her up on my last day as I made my way to the airport.

I told Jane about my plans. She was willing to accommodate my schedule. It would be almost 6:30 pm before I could get to Gretna from the airport. She offered no complaint. Of course it would be fine to show up in the evening, she said. "And my husband is an excellent cook, so he'll make you a fabulous dinner!" I assured her they didn't have to feed me. I commented that it seemed everyone offered to feed us there.

She responded, "Well, yeah, it's kind of a New Orleans thing." I had to laugh. Where else in this country do people offer to feed you dinner when you adopt a cat?

Sandy decided to come with me to meet Nola. When we got there a woman from the neighborhood was waiting on the porch with Jane. Jane explained that the neighbor was so excited when she heard volunteers from California were coming, that she insisted on staying so she could meet us. The neighbor told us she was an expert in reflexology and wanted to give each of us a hand massage as her way of thanking us for helping the community. And so she did -- all the while explaining the benefits of reflexology and thanking us repeatedly for helping Louisiana.

After a while we went inside to meet Nola. She was sitting in a corner and looking perturbed. I approached her slowly and let her smell my hand before attempting to pet her. She didn't look happy at all. Her eyes were narrowed and her ears were down. She had the look a cat gets right before it bites someone. I was losing confidence that she was the cat for my family. I told Sandy later, "That cat was giving me the stink-eye."

But a few minutes later she allowed me to scratch her neck and pet her just a little. I decided to take a chance on her because she needed us. She was already eight months old, no longer a tiny kitten. I'd been told most people only want kittens, so it's hard to find owners for cats who are older. So I paid the adoption fee and made plans to pick her up three days later. Jane offered to waive the adoption fee because she knew I'd done volunteer work at the animal shelter. But I couldn't accept her offer, because I knew she'd spent a lot of her own money to cover the medical costs for all 15 of the cats she was fostering.

The next morning Sandy and I headed to the office of the St. Bernard Project. It was a non-profit organized by a lawyer and a teacher from Washington DC who volunteered in The Parish in the early months after Katrina. The magnitude of the damage in The Parish was so shocking to them, they decided to move there and spearhead a rebuilding program. They kept their operating expenses to a minimum and found corporate sponsors. And because of this efficient management, they were able to completely restore homes for families that had only $10,000 to rebuild. The St. Bernard Project focused on helping elderly and handicapped residents, as well as families with school-age children. Other non-profits were helping the elderly and handicapped, but the SBP was the first I'd heard of that was helping young families too. Sandy and I were impressed with this couple and the personal sacrifices they'd made to rebuild The Parish.

They sent us to a home in Violet that was close to completion. Our team of volunteers would be painting the full interior of the home. There were about ten of us representing several states -- Michigan, Wisconsin, California and Washington DC. Two of the volunteers were a husband and wife team, three others were graduate students. One man just came there on his own, and so did one of the women. We worked efficiently and got the job done within just a few hours.

The owners of the home were a family of four and a grandmother. They were living in a FEMA trailer in the backyard. The mother and grandmother came into the house to thank everyone while we worked. The mother had been working alongside the volunteers for most of the process, but had been told to sit back and let us do the work this time. She told us about the long road they'd taken to recovery -- recalling the weeks of living in a relief shelter and struggling to find relatives they'd lost touch with due to hasty evacuations.

The new plumbing hadn't been completed in the house yet, so the family said we could use the bathroom in their FEMA trailer. Four of the five members of the family were in the trailer, and it was eye opening to see just how cramped it really was when they were in it together. With the exception of that tiny little bathroom, there really was no privacy. The two women were busy in the kitchen area, frying chicken to feed the volunteers for lunch. They were such gracious people, not taking any help for granted.

Sandy and I left soon after the work was completed. We had another mission to accomplish. Two months earlier Sandy and her husband made the decision to purchase a home in St. Bernard. It had already been gutted when they found it. They didn't buy it as an investment. They bought it as a second home, because Sandy knew she wanted to be around people from St. Bernard Parish on a regular basis. Everyone thought they were crazy. They warned them it would cost from $70,000 to $90,000 to complete the repairs. Sandy answered, "I don't care. We'll be making a contribution to the community. It'll be one less destroyed and vacant home." I had been excited to purchase a housewarming present. At first I thought about giving them an axe to keep in the attic -- but decided that was too pessimistic. So I thought of a much better gift -- a Virgin Mary statue for the front yard.

Sandy and I left the home in Violet and headed to her new house to hang curtains. It would probably be a year or two before the work was completed, but for now we could make it look like a normal home from the outside. With curtains up, no one would see that the walls were still exposed wooden beams. One of the other volunteers came with us to see the house, because she was interested in purchasing a home there too.

When we finished with the curtains, we went back to our room in The Quarter to shower and go out for dinner. Afterward we stopped at Lafitte's Blacksmith Shop for Hurricanes. A Hurricane is a specialty drink in New Orleans that tastes like punch. After Katrina, we made it a tradition to drink one each time we visited. It was our silly way of giving Katrina the one-finger salute. But the impact of the drink depended heavily on which bartender made it. Sometimes the drinks went down with minimal damage. But other times they delivered a result similar to that of a Long Island Iced Tea. I guess it didn't help that the drinks came in big tumblers and they hardly tasted like alcohol, so it was easy to drink too much too fast.

Well, this time our Hurricanes were about a category five. Before long we were giggling our way down Bourbon Street. Everything was hilarious. We found a club with a live band that was playing fun music from the 80s and 90s. The females in this club outnumbered the males by about five to one. So a lot of ladies were dancing alone and having a great time. Sandy and I were happily dancing and singing along when two women approached us with big smiles. They were two of the other volunteers who'd been working on the house in Violet. They weren't feeling any pain either. We greeted each other with big hugs. We'd just met them earlier that day but, after sharing the experience of volunteering together, they felt like old friends. The four of us spent the rest of the night dancing and singing.

I am not much of a drinker, so I never bought another drink that night. I was already feeling pretty good from the Hurricane. The problem was that the other three women were buying more drinks and buying them for me, too. I don't know if there was ever a time when I wasn't holding one. I was already so loopy and having so much fun, I didn't pay attention to how many drinks I had.

But something had my attention the next morning -- an unrelenting headache. When I sat up my stomach lurched. I was having my very first hangover. I told you I'm not much of a drinker. Sandy was feeling OK, and the Irish-Italian-Islenos parade would be starting soon. It was the primary reason we'd picked that weekend to be there. But there was no way I could get up and get ready. Sandy ran to the store to get me some aspirin and water and other remedies. I was lucky to have someone with me who knew what I needed. The aspirin helped, but I was moving slowly. I told Sandy to take the rental car and go without me, so she wouldn't miss the beginning of the parade. I'd catch a cab later.

Just before I called for a cab, the phone rang. It was the guesthouse owner, Jay, asking if we needed more towels or toiletries. I told him I'd be catching a cab soon and that I was running late because of my hangover. He laughed and said, "Well it's only fitting that you should have your very first hangover in New Orleans."

I was feeling much better by the time the cab arrived. I recognized my cab driver as one I'd had before. I liked him because he drove sanely and liked to chat. He talked about the frustrations of living in post-Katrina New Orleans. Rents had skyrocketed, demand for cabs was down, and the promised government assistance hadn't arrived. He said, "Everyone I know is tired of the struggle. And all of us are picking up our old vices. I stopped smoking ten years ago, but I've started again. My wife is smoking again too. Lots of friends are drinking much more than they ever did before." It wasn't the first time I'd heard these things. A lot of people confessed they were drinking and eating more after Katrina. They knew it wasn't good for them, but it brought some level of comfort in the trying times.

He dropped me off at the house just in time for the parade. There was a big crowd lined up along the street. We joined them and Molly showed us how to get the float riders' attention by waving our hands in the air and yelling, "Hey, hey, hey!" We had a blast -- catching trinkets, beads, potatoes and carrots. Molly, Sandy and others nearby kept handing me toys they caught and saying, "Take these home to your children." The best part of it all was watching the residents in the crowd and on the floats. This was a rare time when they could put down their hammers, take off their work gloves, and just enjoy the day. They all looked so happy.

After the parade, Molly introduced us to her mother, sister, aunts, cousins and friends. They were all so welcoming. I spent a lot of time with her Aunt Patricia and cousin Wendy. We talked as we ate freshly boiled crawfish. I felt so comfortable with them -- it was like talking with my own relatives. A few people asked if I was the one who'd written about the parade the previous year. I asked them about their Katrina experiences. Aunt Patricia, her husband and father-in-law had sought refuge in a hotel in New Orleans during the storm. It was always surreal to speak to someone who'd been there when Katrina hit. They all seemed so well adjusted, and it was hard to imagine that they were the same people we'd worried about as we watched the news.

Throughout the weekend I'd heard people all over The Parish mention their frustration with the lack of progress on the part of some of the businesses in the area. One building that was particularly frustrating to them was a Taco Bell near The Parish government complex. It was still ungutted, over a year and a half after the flood. I had noticed it too -- it was impossible to miss -- and it was an eyesore. It was on one of the busiest streets in The Parish. The big glass windows had all blown out and people could see straight in to where damaged electrical wires and heating ducts swung in the breeze. There was about a foot of debris and insulation piled on the floor. The strangest thing in the restaurant was a sofa that rested on top of battered dining tables. No one knew where the sofa had come from. Most likely it had floated in from somewhere else. But people were disgusted that the building had been neglected for a year and a half. They wondered why Taco Bell hadn't done something about it.

I'd been asking the same question since the first time I saw that building three months after Katrina. Every time I went back to The Parish, the Taco Bell still looked the same. Other fast food restaurants had at least gutted the interiors or boarded the windows. After I heard how disheartened the residents were about it, I felt compelled to do something. So on our way out of The Parish that day, I told Sandy to pull over at the Taco Bell.

I was angry at Taco Bell's parent company when I pulled out my camcorder. But, just before I started filming, I realized there could be another side to the story. I knew I couldn't go on a verbal tirade against the corporation without knowing all the facts. So while I filmed, I explained what I was showing, but tried to remain as neutral as possible. I knew it was a franchise-owned business. So the responsibility for cleaning and rebuilding would probably fall to the franchisee. However, if the franchisee were a local resident, there was a good chance he'd lost his home too. Maybe all his resources were being used to rebuild his home. But wouldn't the national corporation help in such a situation -- if not out of kindness, then maybe out of self-interest? It certainly wasn't a good public relations strategy to leave the restaurant looking as if it had exploded. I'd personally become so disgusted that I hadn't gone to any Taco Bell restaurants in the previous four months -- because every time I thought of their food, an image of that building popped into my head and I lost my appetite.

So as I filmed I said, "It's really a shame that the corporations can't get out here and at least gut or demolish these buildings…People are trying to come home and rebuild their houses and they have to drive past this Taco Bell every day…I think if the national corporation of Taco Bell knew about this -- which I hope they don't know, because if they do know and they're not fixing this, something's really really wrong. But I would hope that if they knew about this they would gut it or demolish it, so the people who are trying to come back to their towns don't have to look at this destruction for another year and a half." I ended the video by zooming in on fast food restaurants nearby that had gutted and one that had reopened.

And I said, "I wish I knew what the story was with this Taco Bell. And I wish someone would take responsibility for this mess." I wasn't sure what I'd do with the video, but I knew I had to show it to someone.

The next day it was time to go home -- and time to take Nola home with me. I had left a pet carrier at Jane's house and Nola was already inside it when I arrived to pick her up. She and I dropped off the rental car, took the shuttle to the airport and proceeded to the security gate. When I reached the security scanner I asked how Nola would be processed. The security guard said flatly, "You'll have to take the pet out of the carrier, we'll inspect the carrier, and you'll walk through the scanner holding your pet."

I responded, "Uh, this is a cat."

"I'm sorry, that's the procedure."

"I just adopted her today. She's not going to be comforted by me at all."

He looked exasperated. "I'm sorry, that's the way it has to be done."

A woman in line behind me with a local accent said, "Oh that's so nice of you to come here to adopt an animal."

The guard looked at me impatiently and exhaled deeply. I looked at him and said, "OK." But what I was really thinking was, "I hope you understand what we're all in for here and you'll have no one to blame but yourself."

I put the carrier on the floor and started to unzip it. I had visions of the cat clawing me like Freddy Krueger and bolting through the airport to find a dark corner in a storage area to call home for the rest of her life.

The security guard moved closer. "Excuse me, ma'am, do you know how to scruff a cat?"

"What? No."

"Okay, I'm going to help you. Here's what you do." He picked her up by the back of the neck with one hand, supported her body with the other and encouraged me to do the same. Nola went completely still, she didn't fight at all. We went through the scanner and the same guard met us on the other side. Then he took Nola from me and placed her in the carrier.

His voice changed from authoritative to friendly. "I have four cats at home. Don't worry, she'll warm up to you in no time."

Nola and I boarded the plane and she stayed very still and quiet for the entire trip. I was able to put the carrier in my lap and reach in carefully to pet her from time to time. The plane was noisy, especially at take-off and landing. We had a layover in Dallas, and it took about eight hours to get home. I knew she must be terrified.

I hadn't told my family that I was bringing Nola home. I didn't want them to be disappointed if it didn't work out. So I knew this was going to be a fun surprise, at least for the kids. When I got home, my daughters saw two eyes peeking out of the carrier. They were so excited they started screaming -- not exactly the best way to welcome a cat. Nola started hissing and growling. And Jim wasn't as pleasantly surprised as the kids were. But he understood the need for animal adoptions in the New Orleans area, especially after seeing the shelter. So he accepted Nola as our new pet.

Nola spent the next few days hiding under our bed. She'd burrow herself under the center of the bed, too far in to reach with an outstretched arm. She'd watch each one of our movements accusingly with narrowed eyes. I realized she didn't trust us after I put her through that scary plane ride.

She'd stay under the bed all day, hardly moving at all until we turned out the lights and went to sleep. Then we'd wake to the sound of her darting all over the bedroom, apparently getting her exercise and play time while she felt she was safe from us. It was clear this arrangement wasn't going to work.

So I called Jane for advice. She recommended that we give Nola a room of her own to eat, sleep and play in for a week or so as she adapted to the new environment. After a few days, I was able to lure her into the laundry room with some food. She liked it better there because people didn't go into that room as much and she had more time alone. I had to put up a barricade around the dryer because she kept squeezing herself behind it, where there were just a few inches of space, and she'd stay there for hours. I made a bed for her and placed it on top of a counter. But she didn't like it. I could tell she felt too exposed. So I kept one of the cupboard doors open and she would climb in it and make a cozy spot for herself in the back. I gave her a small soft blanket to lie on. At that point she decided this cupboard would be her bedroom. She stayed in the laundry room for a couple weeks, running into the cupboard whenever I came in to feed her, change her litter box or do laundry.

When I was young my family took in a feral cat, and Nola's behavior reminded me of that cat. My childhood cat never completely lost her skittishness, even after years of nurturing.

But she warmed up to us considerably and learned to trust us. Nola had also been born feral and lived that way for the first few months of her life. I'd expected her to be shy and slow to trust, but after about three weeks she did something that had me questioning the adoption.

It was feeding time and I went to the laundry room. As soon as she saw me she glared and hissed. I took it personally. I started to wonder if she'd ever come around and was offended that she was still hostile after weeks of cajoling and feeding. I'd expected that by this point she'd show a little appreciation. I don't know how, maybe by letting me come within five feet of her. I could understand it when she ran and hid, but hissing was just plain rude. "Don't you hiss at me, you little *bleep*," I snapped. I dumped her food into her bowl and stomped out. I'd had it. I went to my room fuming and thinking all kinds of terrible things about her. I wondered if it was safe to have her around my children, concerned she might bite one of them. But after about 20 minutes I calmed down and started to feel sorry for her. She'd been through some scary stuff in her young life. I went quietly back into the laundry room and sat on the floor, and to my surprise, she slowly approached me.

Things didn't change quickly, but every week she became a little braver, a little more trusting. After about three months she started to follow me everywhere. And soon after that she started purring every time she saw me. And that was the only sign of appreciation I really needed. It was quite a compliment actually. A few months later she decided her favorite place to sleep at night was on top of my ankles. It was a little uncomfortable, but very sweet. And she still sleeps there most nights. But sometimes, I wake up to the sound of her purring as she curls up next to my ear on the pillow. And even in my half-dazed state, her presence reminds me that some things get better with time and patience.

CHAPTER EIGHTEEN

God and CNN

The trip in March had been an eventful one, and there were more developments yet to come. I uploaded the video of Taco Bell to YouTube and then posted the link to it on a St. Bernard Parish online message board. Before long, people from The Parish posted comments. Some said thank you, others said they had sent the link to Taco Bell's parent corporation. Someone else said they were sending it to the media. Later I was checking the news on CNN.com and saw a request for viewer videos, so I sent the Taco Bell video to them. I thought if CNN took an interest in the story, they might call Taco Bell with questions. And that might lead to results in The Parish.

The next day there were more messages from residents saying they'd e-mailed and phoned Taco Bell to complain. But Taco Bell sent back a letter to some of them, stating that they'd already gutted and boarded the building. But they were mistaken. The work had been done on a different Taco Bell in a different part of St. Bernard. Someone on the message board copied the text of Taco Bell's letter in his message, so the name and phone number of the corporation's public relations man was at the bottom. I decided to call him, to clarify the location of the restaurant and inform him that it was still in need of repair.

He wasn't available when I called, so I left a message. The woman taking the message was inquisitive and took down my information. I didn't expect to hear back, but a few hours later the PR man called and asked for clarification about the problem. He said the corporation hadn't known the building was in such disrepair because the franchisee had asked The Parish government to demolish the building a year earlier. I told him The Parish government was so busy trying to rebuild the 500 square miles of destruction, that it wasn't surprising they hadn't gotten around to demolishing the building yet. I explained that they were rebuilding The Parish from the ground up -- sewage systems, roads and houses. The Parish government's responsibilities had gone from small town concerns to full-scale disaster recovery overnight.

He told me Taco Bell was embarrassed about the situation, and found it unacceptable. He promised to have someone there "on the ground" within 24 hours to assess the situation and find a solution. He mentioned the video and asked if I'd seen it. I answered sheepishly, "Um, yeah, I filmed it." I explained my reasons and told him I'd hoped they'd do something about it if they saw it for themselves. I told him people were becoming angry at Taco Bell for the state of that building, regardless of who was responsible.

I have to give him credit -- he was good at his job. He tried to explain the corporation's position on the issue without becoming defensive. And he was very apologetic. I told him my goal was to see that the building was cleaned up, not to humiliate Taco Bell. And so I would remove the video when the work was done. He asked if, in the meantime, I'd add a statement to the video explaining that they were working on the problem. And he asked if I'd add his name and e-mail address as a contact for anyone who had questions or concerns. I asked, "Are you sure you want to do that?" I imagined he might get some angry messages. But he assured me that was what he wanted. So I edited the video as he requested.

That conversation took place on a Wednesday, one day after I uploaded the original video to YouTube. On Friday morning, I found a message from a Parish resident saying he'd just gone by the Taco Bell and he'd seen two men working on the building. Later that day, someone posted a message that said the building had been boarded up. And so, since the PR man kept his word, I kept mine. I removed the video from YouTube's public access that same day.

Earlier that morning I met my friend Donna for coffee. She was one friend who'd asked a lot about what I'd seen in The Parish. So I brought pictures and told her all about St. Bernard. She was stunned by all the stories, surprised more hadn't been said about The Parish in the media. She said I should write to Oprah. I told her I already had -- four or five times -- with no success. I'd written to the New York Times and Washington Post -- nothing. She said there must be someone who'd help tell the story. Maybe Sean Penn or Spike Lee. I thought about it. Maybe I should write to them. But I was feeling discouraged. It seemed like the media had lost interest -- they claimed the public had "Katrina Fatigue." Anderson Cooper was one of the only national media figures who continued to share what was happening in the Katrina Zone. I loved what he said on more than one occasion -- that the only people who could legitimately claim to have Katrina Fatigue were the people who lived in the Katrina zone.

When I got home from meeting with Donna, I found the first of the messages that described the work happening on the Taco Bell in The Parish. Later in the afternoon I picked my girls up from school. I told them Taco Bell was working on the building, and they cheered. I was so excited, I felt like I'd won the lottery. I drove to Taco Bell for the first time in four months and bought burritos and nachos to celebrate. On the way home I talked to my girls about The Parish residents and how they'd influenced Taco Bell by writing, calling and making their feelings known. But it felt strange that I didn't know any of their real names, since everyone had user names on the message board.

A couple hours later the phone rang. The Caller ID showed an unfamiliar area code. I answered the phone expecting a telemarketer. But the voice on the other end said, "Hello, this is Mike from CNN. I'm calling about the Taco Bell video."

After I got over the initial shock my first thought was, "Oh crap, I'm getting Taco Bell in trouble with the media and they've already done the work!" I'd honestly forgotten that I'd sent the video to CNN. I'd been sending video of The Parish to various media sources for the previous year and a half and had only heard back from the local CBS news station. I told Mike that Taco Bell was working on the building that very day. He sounded surprised. I imagined he must have been thinking the story was a bust. But he kept asking questions.

The conversation led to the subject of the overall recovery of The Parish. I explained the frustration I had with the lack of media coverage there. Why were the reporters always standing in the Lower 9th Ward when there were places like St. Bernard Parish, Plaquemines Parish, New Orleans East, Lakeview and Gentilly with equal or more extensive damage? I wanted the

Lower 9th Ward to get help -- they needed it. But other areas needed it too. I told him of my experience there during the first post-Katrina Spring, when St. Bernard Parish didn't have the seven volunteers it needed to run the relief center, but the Lower 9th Ward -- just a few blocks away -- had three to four thousand volunteers that same week.

Mike kept asking questions and I kept answering. I have to admit I was surprised that he was listening. He told me it was a compelling story and he'd like for me to give them an interview for a new show called News To Me. He said I'd hear from them again in a week or two. But I didn't. I was a little disappointed and a little relieved. The idea of giving an interview for a national program was a bit daunting.

A few weeks later I went with my sister and mother to a lecture by successful author and speaker Marianne Williamson. She had been an inspiration to me for many years. I'd heard her say once that when a problem exists in the world, the people who get the most depressed about it are the ones who don't do anything to contribute to the solution. That statement stuck with me, and it was one of the thoughts that motivated me to go to St. Bernard Parish and New Orleans after Katrina.

After the lecture she took comments and questions, so I decided to thank her for that statement. Then I commented that my sister and I had been trying to get the word out that there were still communities affected by Katrina that hardly anyone knew about, and they still needed help. But we weren't seeing much in terms of results. I expressed that this was very frustrating for us. I did not expect the answer she gave me. She said I needed to accept that the solution might not happen in my lifetime. I smiled and thanked her, but inside I was thinking, "Oh yes it will!"

Later my mother, sister and I talked about it. I told them I absolutely believed The Parish would get the recognition it needed in my lifetime. I wasn't willing to give up, and I intended to keep working on it until it happened. But I'd also come to accept that it didn't have to come through me. I'd realized I couldn't make it about my own ego. It didn't really matter to me who made it happen. But I also knew that, until it happened, I had to keep working toward that goal. My sister asked me to define my goal. So I told her it was to see The Parish get so much support and so many volunteers that the residents would be able to say, "OK, enough. Thank you, everyone -- now please go home."

It was an important turning point for me when I accepted that I didn't have to be the hero that made change happen, as long as I didn't give up. I held on to hope that CNN would do a story on The Parish and it didn't matter if I was involved or not, as long as their story was told.

Not long after, I saw a poll in the New Orleans Times-Picayune. It questioned residents of local areas about their plans for the future and their levels of optimism about recovery. It showed St. Bernard Parish residents were the least optimistic. I understood why -- they lived in one of the areas that was getting the least amount of help. I e-mailed the poll to Mike at CNN with a note that it was just more evidence that St. Bernard Parish needed more media attention to attract more help.

I didn't expect to hear back from him. But he wrote back, saying the new show had been delayed, but they were still interested in doing an interview. I was nervous. I didn't want it to turn into a rant against Taco Bell -- they'd boarded up the building. Some people may have felt it should have happened sooner, some thought they should have done more. But others were happy about the situation. And I was grateful that they'd responded so quickly to the video.

In the days leading up to the interview I prayed that the show would give St. Bernard Parish some needed exposure around the country. It was pointless to do the show unless some good came out of it. So I prayed that God and CNN would find a way to cancel the interview if the story wouldn't bring about some positive change for The Parish.

I called Molly the night before the interview. I wanted to get her feedback on how things were going in The Parish. I felt better after talking with her. We discussed how much progress The Parish had made since Katrina, and how much help they could still use from outside sources.

The next day I was contacted by Eric, the host of CNN's News To Me show. I was relieved to hear him say he didn't want to focus too much on the Taco Bell story. He was more interested in asking about other issues. I told him that was good because I was more interested in talking about the other issues. We scheduled a time to conduct the interview. He told me he'd read the letter I'd sent to friends that ended up on the KPIX San Francisco web site, and he'd found it interesting. Sometimes I think about that letter -- it started as my small way of sharing St. Bernard's story with friends. I'd been so depressed when there was no immediate response, but then it wound up in the hands of KPIX and CNN. It took me about four hours to write that letter, because I couldn't stop crying while I was typing it and remembering the people I'd left behind in The Parish.

The night before the interview I told Gabrielle I couldn't believe I'd be giving CNN an interview the next day. I told her

I was trying not to think about it too much because I'd get too nervous. I said I didn't know many people who'd ever been interviewed by CNN. But then realized I didn't know anyone who ever had. My daughter just smiled and said, "Mom, stop thinking about it."

The interview went smoothly -- Eric was adept at putting his guests at ease. He kept the focus on the overall recovery of The Parish. CNN had requested some of the video I'd taken of The Parish to use in the story, too. So I was glad the video might be put to good use. When the interview was over, the associate producer told me the show would be on in a few weeks and they'd notify me before it aired.

CHAPTER NINETEEN

Buck and Molly's California Adventure

In June we made plans for some very special guests. Molly and Buck had decided to take a much-needed break from rebuilding. Sandy and I had been nagging them for months to come to California. Before Katrina, they'd planned to take a big trip to celebrate their 25th wedding anniversary. But Katrina had sidelined those plans. When we visited them in March 2007, we were finally able to convince them to get away from it all for a little while. Sandy offered to be their unofficial travel agent, and she laid out an itinerary that included visits to her home and to mine. They'd stay with Sandy for a few days, then head to San Francisco. A few days later, I'd meet them there and bring them to my home. And then they'd go to Pismo Beach for a weekend. My whole family was excited. They'd fallen in love with Buck and Molly just like I had.

As I prepared for their visit, I tried to find souvenirs from my hometown to give them. My city is known for its vineyards and wineries, so I wanted to get some good bottles of local wine. I entered the tasting room of one of my favorite places and waited as the customer ahead of me tasted wines and conversed with the woman behind the counter. When I ordered three bottles, the two women asked if I was preparing for a special occasion. I told them we had friends visiting from the New Orleans area.

The woman tasting wine engaged me in a conversation about New Orleans and Katrina. She said she had friends in the area, and had heard the rebuilding process was moving slowly. Then she told me how she met those friends. She had been in New Orleans on vacation with her husband when they met a local couple. The local couple had been friendly and hospitable and had even invited this woman and her husband to their home for a jambalaya dinner. She said, "But they weren't from New Orleans, they were from a suburb a few miles away."

I know there are many suburbs near New Orleans, but I had a feeling I knew where that couple lived. I asked, "St. Bernard Parish?"

"Yeah, how did you know?"

"That's where my friends are from too."

For a moment we looked at each other, wondering if we'd met the same couple, but we hadn't. But it didn't really surprise me to hear about other hospitable people from The Parish. And it was interesting that, halfway across the country, people from the same small community had befriended both of us.

By the time Buck and Molly arrived, the CNN show still hadn't aired and I was a little disappointed. But I reminded myself that it would air when it was meant to. And if it didn't air at all, there must be a good reason for it. The associate producer had told me he'd send an e-mail before they ran the show, and I hadn't heard anything.

We had a great visit with Buck and Molly. It was fun to see them enjoying some time off, after a year and a half of constant working and rebuilding. No one deserved a vacation more than they did. They had a great time in San Francisco, taking in all the famous sights. I met them there and brought them home where Jim was waiting. He'd taken the day off of work to spend more time with them. Later in the evening my parents and friends, Nancy and Fred, came over to join us for dinner. They'd heard a lot about Buck and Molly and were eager to meet them.

When the other guests had gone and Gabrielle and Claire were tucked into bed, Buck showed us a video he'd brought from home. It was footage of the first day they'd been allowed back in The Parish after the flood. The beginning of the video showed a huge line of cars, bumper to bumper, waiting to get back into The Parish. The cars were full of people who were finally going to see what Katrina had done to their homes and communities. It had taken so long for the water to recede, that almost a full month had passed since the flood.

Buck had brought his video camera and filmed as they discovered what remained of their house and their parents' houses. In some shots we could see Molly quietly walking through her home, assessing the damage and trying to figure out where items had floated. There were no hysterics, just shocked silence. At some points the only thing we could hear was the sound of the dried mud crunching under their shoes. It was difficult to watch our friends in that devastating moment and try to imagine what was going through their minds. But I felt honored that they were willing to share it with us -- especially because they often avoided sharing any sad stories. They didn't see any point in dwelling on the hard times.

On Friday, Sandy and her husband Keith stopped at our house to pick up Molly and Buck and take them to Pismo Beach. Originally Jim, the girls and I hadn't planned on going because it was the last day of school. But we changed our minds at the last minute. I got on the phone and hoped to find an available room in Pismo. We lucked out and found a place just a few blocks from where Sandy had made reservations. The weather was nice in Pismo and we all had a great time that weekend, playing on the beach. We rented wetsuits and Boogie Boards and rode the waves for hours.

I wanted to watch News To Me on Saturday morning, just in case my interview was on. I didn't expect it to be, but didn't want to miss it if it was. My family's hotel didn't get CNN's Headline News channel. So I asked Sandy if we could watch it in her room. We were running late, but I wasn't really concerned because it wasn't supposed to be on anyway. We knocked on Sandy's door just as the show was starting. We waited a long time and then we could hear her yelling on the other side of the door, "It's on, it's on, it's on!"

She threw the door open, and we ran inside to watch. Sandy grabbed the phone and called Molly. A few seconds later, Molly came in to watch. Michael at CNN had told me the story would only be about 3 minutes long. By the time Molly came in, it was almost half over. But it was another taste of synchronicity -- what were the odds that CNN would interview me about The Parish and then air the story during the one time someone from The Parish was visiting? And something else made it even more rewarding -- the video CNN used included footage of Buck and Molly's daughter Erin. I'd sent them about an hour's worth of video, and in the editing process they'd chosen the only footage I had of Erin, which was about three seconds long.

When we came home, I found an e-mail that Michael at CNN had sent on Friday, telling me the interview would air the next day. I'd already left for Pismo Beach when he sent it. I regretted that I hadn't been able to e-mail friends to let them know it would be on. But I guess that would have been for my own ego. And I'd already realized that what mattered was that the story was told -- not who told it. The most important thing was that CNN had shed some light on what was happening in The Parish.

CHAPTER TWENTY

Watchdogs

I wanted to be back in New Orleans and The Parish on the second anniversary of Katrina. I know that seems weird. But I knew there'd be ceremonies to honor the survivors and commemorate those who didn't survive. I wanted to be there to acknowledge the significance of what had happened.

My family was eager to go back too. They'd all been envious when I went back to The Parish in March with Sandy. Before they'd been to Louisiana, they would send me off on my trips with hugs and wishes for safe travel. But after they'd been there, they also sent me off with protests, "How come we can't go too?" So we decided to go back as a family again and make it our trip for summer vacation. But the kids' first day of school would be August 29th -- the anniversary of Katrina. Since we wouldn't be able to be there for the second anniversary, we scheduled our trip for a week earlier.

I started checking out private condos in The Quarter for rent. We needed to keep costs down since all the trips were eating into our savings. I found a condo that might be within our budget, $125 per night. But when I wrote to the owner for more information, I learned that was the cost for two people. The cost for four people was $160 dollars. It was too much. I wrote back, telling her we had chosen the place based on the $125 price, because we were coming to volunteer in St. Bernard Parish and needed to keep our costs down. Was it possible to get it for $125 dollars?

Her response surprised me. She said she had to fight back tears when she read my message because she had once lived in St. Bernard Parish. Yes, she would absolutely lower the rental fee for us. She asked, "How does $75 a night sound?" I was stunned. She had just dropped her price by more than half! It was too low, and I didn't want to take advantage of anyone there. But I also didn't want to offend her. I'd learned from experience that it's uplifting to help someone you really want to help. To have the offer denied is deflating. I wrote to her with a compromise, how about $100 per night? She wrote back, "If the $100 makes you and your family feel better, of course, that's fine. I always believe what goes around comes around, and it will come back to me in many ways."

I was overwhelmed by her generosity. But she surprised me even more when she wrote a few days later to say she'd talked with some friends and they'd decided to raise money for the St. Bernard Parish Animal Shelter in honor of my family. She and her friends were members of the Slidell Newcomers Club and many of them had a soft spot for St. Bernard. A lot of St. Bernard residents had relocated to Slidell after Katrina destroyed their homes in The Parish. She asked if we'd be willing to meet some of her friends at the shelter when they dropped off the donations. We were absolutely willing to meet them and see what they brought for the animals.

I e-mailed Mike at CNN to tell him I'd be back there just before the anniversary. I figured they'd be covering the New Orleans area again and I hoped they'd include St. Bernard's story too. He said it would be great if I could get interviews with residents, asking them about their recovery experiences. I tried to brainstorm -- who would be a good person to interview? Then I remembered Mark Madary, the Parish councilman who'd brought bottled water to Sandy and me while we planted flowers on the neutral ground. He'd be a great resource for information about the recovery process. So I called him to ask if he'd be willing to give me an interview. I told him I was from California, and that I'd met him when I was in The Parish a year or so earlier. He asked, "Are you one of the two women who planted flowers on the neutral ground?"

I couldn't believe he remembered me. He agreed to an interview and told me to call when I arrived to schedule a time. So, once again, I packed my video camera.

Jim and I signed up to work with The St. Bernard Project. We had to take turns though, since one of us would need to watch the kids while the other worked. On our first full day there we dropped Jim off at a house in Violet, where he would be spackling and painting for the day.

I made arrangements to meet with Councilman Madary while Jim worked. The girls and I picked him up in a borrowed truck and he gave us a tour of The Parish. We stopped frequently to shoot video and conduct pieces of the interview. He was a wealth of information. Since he was a Parish councilman, he knew all the important numbers. He told us only about 35 - 40% of the residents had moved back and most of the residents hadn't received any of the money allocated by Congress to help them rebuild. They had to rebuild with their own money. He said, "I understand there's been $116 billion dollars allocated to the storm. I'd like to know whose checking account that money's in. It has not filtered to the local government. The state government supposedly is holding some. The rest of it they said it's for the state to ask the federal government for it. So whoever's not asking, please do so. Because, you can see, in most people's cases they have not moved forward with their lives because they have not received the assistance that was promised."

He showed us a house that had been condemned for involuntary demolition, because it had been sitting in a destroyed state for two years and efforts had not been made to restore it. I asked what would happen if there were enough volunteers to rebuild it. He answered, "This house could be saved."

But he told me they were grateful for the volunteers who had come to The Parish, saying they were largely responsible for the progress that had taken place. "If it hadn't been for the heart and the soul of the people from across the United States wanting to help, nothing would be possible."

Mark took us to the flood-damaged home where he and his siblings had been raised. It was in a mostly deserted neighborhood in Arabi where only about 15% of the homeowners had returned. When the camera was off he showed us the rooftop where he'd been stranded during the flood, after the vehicle he'd been in was swept away by floodwater. He told me the water was so high that when he swam he was at the same level as the power lines.

Mark stayed with us for almost three hours, doing his best to get the word out about the parish he loved. Afterward, the girls and I stopped at Rocky and Carlos restaurant to pick up muffulettas for lunch, then took one to Jim. Then we needed to get to the animal shelter to meet the ladies from The Slidell Newcomers Club.

The heat and humidity that day were stifling. The ladies had arrived early and had already unloaded most of their donations -- two van loads full of pet beds, food and toys. We were amazed. Then they handed the shelter director a check for $200. Her huge smile indicated the donations were deeply appreciated. The Slidell ladies asked my daughters and me to take a photo with them and the shelter director. We all paused briefly for a few photos, but everyone was anxious to get back inside a car, building or FEMA trailer where there'd be air conditioning. The ladies submitted the photo to The Picayune newspaper and, when it was published, they mailed a copy to our home.

The next day it was my turn to work on a house. I was up for the challenge -- excited and ready to go. When we got the address of the house I was even more pleased. It was one block away from Molly and Buck's house. What a privilege it would be to work in their neighborhood after all the kindness and generosity they'd shown. But when we went inside the house it was clear that the work being done was something Jim was more qualified to do -- installing baseboards and window trim. I had to grapple with a choice. I knew I would get immense satisfaction from doing the work, but Jim would do it better. I could see Jim wanted to stay. He told me he'd love to do the work, but he wouldn't horn in on my chance if it would upset me. So I asked myself, what would bring the greatest benefit to the family who owned the house -- Jim's work or mine? It wasn't hard to figure out the answer, so the girls and I left Jim there for a second full day of rebuilding.

The three of us went back to the animal shelter to help feed the dogs and take a few for walks. I asked if I should take video of the animals again. Tina, the director, told me a volunteer had been taking photos of the dogs and posting them online. I was happy other people were interested in helping the shelter -- it clearly needed it. The building that housed the animals had been flooded. Although the electricity had been restored, there was still no air conditioning. The cats were gasping from the heat. The shelter staff did their best to cool the animals. Most of the cages had fans in front of them to keep the air circulating and provide some relief. Tina said they had some new dogs she'd like me to film. But I couldn't resist the other animals, so I filmed all of them.

When we were done, we took a drive through the Lexington Place neighborhood again. There was something that always drew me to that neighborhood. It was where I'd met the woman with the snakes in her pool, the man with the snakes in his garage, the teenage girl with a brick house in her front yard, and the woman with the "KEN" marking on her house. I think part of what drew me there was that it was plain to see this had once been a beautiful neighborhood.

I had the video of Councilman Madary to send to CNN, but there was something else I wanted to capture. I wanted to show this neighborhood and the word "KEN" that had been painted on the houses -- because it was a stark reminder of the severity of what happened here. It was too important to just forget.

I parked the truck and, as I was getting ready to film an abandoned house with the "KEN" marking, I noticed a woman exiting the house next door. Whenever I filmed in The Parish I had ambivalent feelings. I didn't want to offend the residents and behave like an ambulance chaser. They were trying to hold on to the hope that things were getting better and that The Parish was still a wonderful place to live. I knew some people resented when others focused only on the destruction. It was understandable, I'm sure I'd feel the same way. But I knew it was important to capture the images and share the story. I wanted to document it before it disappeared forever -- while there was still some proof of it. Once the houses were demolished or painted over, there would be no evidence of what had happened. And who would ever believe it had happened if they never saw it on the news?

That was one of the hard lessons I learned from Katrina and St. Bernard Parish. We think if something so monumental happened anywhere in this country, surely we'd all know about it, right? I realized we treat our news media like a watchdog group. We expect them to catch every disaster and every crooked politician, every crime or injustice. But we forget that news stations are businesses and are guided in their decisions by profits. And their profits are determined by viewer interest. If the viewers won't be interested in a story, there's a pretty good chance it won't show up on the news. It has to be compelling, shocking, sexy or funny -- just like our TV dramas and sitcoms -- otherwise people won't watch. And a news story can't offend the leaders of any corporation that sponsors the news show's broadcasting company. And if a reporter points a finger at anyone in high places with powerful lawyers, then the story needs to be handled very delicately or completely scratched.

When I came to this realization I was outraged for about ten seconds, until I acknowledged that we have no right to expect a business run for profit to be a watchdog group. In fact, we're probably lucky to have the relatively unbiased news we get from most stations. But now I know that very important stories go untold every day. Ask anyone you know outside Louisiana where the largest residential oil spill in United States history occurred, and they probably can't tell you -- because they never saw it on the news. But in St. Bernard Parish they lived it. I know it's true because I saw it, and my friends Buck and Molly lived in one of the homes destroyed by it. So now, when I watch a reporter standing in the debris field of a tornado-wrecked neighborhood, I find myself wondering how the neighborhoods in the less populated towns nearby fared. So I go to The Parish with my video camera and hope that YouTube will help tell the story. And sometimes CNN or CBS will, too -- if they think the rest of us will watch.

The woman in Lexington Place looked at me and smiled. We walked toward each other, and I told her who I was and what I was doing in her neighborhood. I explained I'd be sending some video to CNN in the hope they'd air it on the Katrina anniversary. She welcomed me as if there was nothing unusual about a stranger videotaping her neighborhood. I told my girls to hop out of the truck and we all stood on the woman's lawn while we talked about the recovery process. She took us inside her house, where two men were doing some repairs. She told me it was hard to find reliable people to do the work at reasonable costs. I'd heard this from a lot of other people too. In a Parish where 27,000 homes and thousands of businesses needed to be rebuilt, the demand for contractors, carpenters, electricians and plumbers far exceeded the supply.

We walked back out to her lawn and continued talking for about ten minutes. The more I talked with her, the more I felt she was the kind of person I would call a friend back home. Even in this time of struggle, she had a smile that came easily and a good sense of humor.

The heat and humidity were stifling. I'd been warned that it was bad this time of year, but words couldn't really explain it. Standing outside felt like standing in a sauna. And I was struck by the realization that this was precisely the type of weather that followed Katrina. I no longer questioned how so many people died of heat stroke in their attics. Now I wondered how anyone in an attic or trapped on a rooftop survived at all.

As I prepared to film the house next door with the "KEN" marking, I had an idea. I asked if she'd be willing to be interviewed. She looked a little reticent at first, glancing down at her work clothes and touching her hair that had been pulled back. I was prepared for her to decline, knowing how most women don't like their picture taken when they haven't had a little time to primp. But she shrugged off any concern she might have had and said she'd do it.

I asked if it was OK to send the video to CNN and other news sources, and to post it on the Internet, and she agreed. The interview she gave me was fantastic. She was smart, well spoken and personable. And she looked like someone everyone knows. Her descriptions of life after Katrina were some of the most heart-felt I'd ever heard.

She showed me a telephone pole that had been marked with a line to indicate the height of the floodwater. The line was so high, I couldn't fit her face and the line in the same frame of my camera.

She said the volunteers had made all the difference. They'd offered assistance and comfort. I asked what she'd recommend people do if they wanted to help. She answered, "Show they care without pitying us. Just care." It was the one thing people from The Parish seemed to want most.

I was holding the camera and asking questions while the dampness of the humidity dripped off my face. My children were melting in the heat, too. They were pulling on me and resting on my arm, as I tried to keep the camera still. They wanted to get back in the truck so I could turn on the air conditioning. But what this woman was telling me was too powerful to interrupt.

When we finished the interview we chatted a little while longer. But I had to get my kids out of that heat. As we prepared to leave, she asked when I'd be back in The Parish. I told her my next trip would be in two to three months. She said, "Then please stop by to see me again -- really, please. My house should be finished by then and I'd really like to be able to offer you something to drink next time." As with so many other residents in St. Bernard, hospitality was essential no matter what the circumstances.

We were invited to Molly and Buck's house for dinner that night, and just about every other night we were there. We always had a great time at their house, but we didn't feel right about sponging off them. We tried to politely decline their invitations a few times, thinking they'd probably welcome a break from playing host and hostess. We didn't want to wear out our welcome. But they didn't like taking no for an answer. One night we invited them to dinner at Nola, one of Emeril Lagasse's restaurants in The Quarter. When the bill came, Buck tried to grab it, but we didn't let him. We argued that they had to allow us to pay for dinner at least one night.

One evening Molly arranged for all of us to take a drive to Bayou LaLoutre, so she could teach Gabrielle and Claire to catch blue crabs. We were joined by their daughter Katey and Molly's sister Cathy, too. And Molly's brother Buddy brought the nets. We all took turns baiting the nets, throwing them out and then pulling them back in and unloading the crabs into a bucket. It was an experience like none we'd ever had before and we all had a great time. We watched fishing vessels pass by as night approached, headed in with their catch for the day. One of the boats idled up to us and a man pointed at a gunnysack half-full of freshly caught oysters. He asked if we wanted them. Jim waited for Buck's response, expecting there'd be some wheeling and dealing to establish a price. But Buck just nodded his head and the man on the boat handed the sack to us and drove away.

Jim couldn't believe it. At home in California, oysters were an expensive delicacy reserved for special occasions. Not here. Buck and Molly explained that the fishermen sell oysters by the gunnysack -- anything less than a full sack is difficult to sell. So the fisherman had given the oysters to us at no charge, rather than see them go to waste. Late that evening we returned to Molly and Buck's house and gorged ourselves on crab and oysters.

Another night we were invited over for the biggest dinner I've ever had. The kitchen had been restored and Molly made a yummy potato salad and a spinach and artichoke soup. Molly and I battered fresh fish, shrimp and oysters. And the men fried them outside in a big propane pot. They made french-fries too. My favorite part of all was when Molly taught me to make fried pickles. Fried pickles! I'd never had them before, but they were delicious. I started thinking about buying a fryer so I could make all these incredible foods at home. And then I asked myself, "What is wrong with you?" In the two years following Katrina I'd gained 20 pounds, and I hold Buck and Molly responsible for at least ten of them.

On our last night with them they gave us the Holy Grail of Louisiana -- old family recipes for gumbo and red beans and rice. Then they handed us two bags full of the necessary spices and ingredients for each dish. We told them they'd done too much, once again. Molly responded, "We're fixing you for not letting us pay at the restaurant the other night."

A few months after we came home I was sorting through Claire's school papers when I came across a writing assignment. The typing at the top of the page said, "The Best Time I Ever Had Was..." and Claire had written this: "The best time I ever had was when me and my family learned how to catch crabs in Louisiana with our friends Molly and Buck."

I made a copy and sent it to Molly. The next time I visited her, she showed me a wall hanging in her hallway. She had framed Claire's assignment and added a photo of her holding a crab at Bayou LaLoutre.

When we got home from that trip I edited the videos I'd taken of Councilman Madary, the lady in Lexington Place and the animal shelter. I posted all the videos on YouTube and sent the first two to CNN. On August 29th, the second anniversary of Katrina, I received a phone call asking if I'd be willing to give CNN Headline News a live interview. I was nervous, but happy that there'd be coverage of The Parish on the news. It would be a phone interview without camera coverage, so that took some of the pressure off. CNN would be showing some of the video I'd sent, while Christi Paul interviewed me by phone.

Christi Paul asked what I thought the most vital need was for those who were trying to rebuild. I told her what they needed most was the Road Home money that had been promised by the government, so they could afford to rebuild. But they also needed volunteers to help with the work. "If you can imagine what it's like to rebuild entire cities...there isn't enough manpower out there... they need more than just money. They need people out there to do the work."

At the end, they played part of my interview with the woman in Lexington Place. At one point I had told her that some people around the country wondered why anyone who'd been through as much as they had would go back to The Parish. When I asked her about it, I already understood why. But I wanted other people to understand, too. She answered, "That is a good question...to be near family. Because it's the life we know and love."

CNN showed pieces of that interview in Lexington throughout the day. I was grateful that CNN was keeping The Parish in the news -- maybe it would inspire people to volunteer there. I tried to keep my eye on the TV whenever I was home. I didn't see the interview with Mark Madary, and I was a little disappointed because he'd provided such good information. But later I was pleasantly surprised when I heard CNN Headline News conducting a live telephone interview with him. And in the evening, Sandy called and said, "I was working out at the gym at lunch time today, and I looked up and there was Mark Madary on CNN!" They'd used the video after all.

Later Oprah Winfrey highlighted the Katrina recovery process. Anderson Cooper and Dr. Oz were her guests because both had been in the Katrina zone in the early days of the flood. Both said there was still an immense need for help there. Anderson shared an interview he'd conducted with Zack Rosenberg and

Liz McCartney, the founders of The St. Bernard Project. He said their organization was a prime example of a volunteer group that was doing things right. Throughout the week I saw several other TV programs that mentioned The Parish. And I was so happy to see they'd been remembered. Finally. But there was still a long way to go.

CHAPTER TWENTY-ONE

A Woman's Place...

After the trip with my family, I wanted to get back to The Parish again soon to help rebuild. I think the longing was heightened by the fact that I hadn't had a chance to do any repair work while I was there with my family.

Jim's office gave us some great news and suddenly our financial situation improved. I was grateful that I wouldn't have to scrounge for nickels and quarters to fund my next trip to New Orleans. Since we'd all been pinching pennies for the previous two years, Jim suggested each of us be allowed to spend a chunk of change on something we really wanted. He wanted a wide screen TV. I was secretly thrilled that he picked something expensive, because it justified the expense of what I wanted -- trips, trips and more trips!

I talked to Sandy about going back with me, but she had already scheduled a trip there with her husband to work on their new home. I had a scheduling conflict and couldn't go at the same time. It became clear that I'd have to go alone if I wanted to go back soon. I welcomed the idea. I thought it would be liberating to be there on my own terms, not worrying about anyone else's agenda. I was a little nervous, but figured I knew the area well enough by that point to avoid any dangerous neighborhoods or situations. And I knew Buck and Molly lived nearby and I could rely on them if I had an emergency. But it turned out Molly was going to be out of town that weekend. I was relieved when she assured me that Buck would be around and I could call him if I needed anything.

I'd gained about 20 pounds since my first post-Katrina trip -- I was eating too well on my visits to Louisiana, and taking that habit home with me. So after The Feast of the Fried Pickles I joined a weight loss program. By the time I was headed back to New Orleans I'd lost eight pounds. I made an appointment with one of the diet counselors a few days before my solo trip because I knew I'd need help boosting my willpower. And I wanted to pick up some diet plan food to pack in my suitcase. But when I told the counselor where I was going she said, "Oh, listen, if you're going to New Orleans just let yourself eat. That food's too good to pass up. Just eat a sensible breakfast and lunch, but you have to have some good New Orleans food for dinner." Now that was a diet plan I could stick with.

I took a red-eye flight and only slept briefly and restlessly on the plane for about two hours. It was the first time I'd tried a red-eye and it's probably the last. I was exhausted when I arrived. I unloaded my suitcases and made a beeline for Central Grocery to order a muffuletta sandwich. Then I drove my rental car to The Parish and stopped at a non-profit office to see if they could use some help the next day. They said they'd have a job for me if I returned early the next morning.

So I drove to my sister's house in Meraux. She'd been there with her husband Keith just two weeks before, repairing their new home. They'd planted two trees in front of the house and Sandy had asked if I would check on them to be sure they were getting enough water. The backyard of her house was on the edge of a marshy wooded area. The foliage was thick, too thick to really walk through. And you wouldn't want to walk through it anyway, because it was filled with debris that had blown or floated there during Katrina. There was no telling what might still be in there.

About one fourth of the houses on her street had been rebuilt. The rest were abandoned, demolished or in the process of being rebuilt. As I drove out of her neighborhood I noticed one of the abandoned houses had a message painted on the front, "Welcome to My Nightmare." I realized I'd driven past that house on the way in and hadn't even noticed it.

I went back to several neighborhoods I'd seen before. I often went past homes where I'd met people on earlier trips, to see what kind of progress they were making. Sometimes the home would be completely gone, demolished with nothing left but a slab. It was always unexpected and always made me sad, because it meant a family had lost a place that had been central to their past. This time I saw something beautiful. It was the home that once had a brick house in the front yard, on the street where Sandy and I had met the two teenagers who'd been locked out of their car. The brick house was gone, but the home that had been behind it was beautifully restored. The yard was nicely landscaped and manicured. Cars were parked in the driveway, so the family had clearly moved back in. And it was so nice to know the teenage girl we'd met had her home again -- especially because the scene in her front yard had been one of the most shocking post-Katrina sights.

I called Buck to ask if he needed help with his house repairs. He said he didn't, but Johnny might -- he was rebuilding his home in the oil spill zone. So I called Johnny and offered to help. But he thought I should help someone less fortunate. "I feel like I don't deserve it," he said. He was doing all right financially, and didn't want to take help away from someone who was struggling to pay for repairs.

So on Saturday morning I reported to the non-profit office. I was greeted by a volunteer who handed me a sheet of paper with the address of the house I'd be working on. I couldn't help but smile when I saw I was being sent to another house close to Buck and Molly's. The volunteer started to give me directions, but I didn't need them. I knew exactly how to get there.

When I got to the house a small celebration was taking place. Two volunteers were helping the residents plant the first tree in the yard since Katrina. The residents were an elderly man and his middle-age son. The son explained that they were replacing a tree that had been blown down by Katrina's winds. The tree was the first Katrina casualty at their home. Gardening had been his father's passion before Katrina, but he'd been too depressed since Katrina to do it anymore. The son said they'd been in the house when the storm hit. They saw a 10-foot wall of water raging down the street toward them and they scrambled to get into the attic with their dogs. He said, "My mamma was sick before Katrina, but we lost her in the storm. My dad had a really hard time with it. I hadn't seen him smile since then -- until your group came to rebuild his house. Now he's smiling again and even teasing me. It's good to see that in him again."

The volunteers that day would be installing wood laminate flooring in the living room and kitchen. There were only three of us, all women. One of the women had been working on the house for several weeks. She had already done some floor work in the house, so she taught us what to do. It was a fun challenge, since we were using a table saw and a chop saw to cut the boards. I'd never used saws before. It felt empowering learning to use new tools and making some kind of long-term improvement to this home. When Sandy had been in The Parish a few weeks before, she and Molly volunteered at a special event The St. Bernard Project sponsored called The Women's Build. Women from all over the country participated and it was a big success. They promoted the event with the slogan, "A Woman's Place is Rebuilding the Home." I loved that slogan and thought of it as we worked on this house.

The younger man of the two residents was recovering from surgery, so he was unable to help with the work. He could only stand for short periods of time, but it didn't stop him from bringing food to us from his FEMA trailer in the front yard.

There were two dogs in the backyard. A couple times a volunteer accidentally left a door or gate open and one of the dogs escaped. Each time, I ran to the front yard to track down the dog. The younger resident thanked me repeatedly. He told me the dog had been with him during the flood. He said,

"After surviving that storm with this dog, I don't know what I'd do if I lost him now." He described swimming through the water as the dog rode on his back, with his paws wrapped around his owner's neck.

The man went quiet for a minute and then asked, "Do you know my story?"

I was glad he asked because I wanted to know his story, but didn't want to be too intrusive. I told him I'd heard a little of what he'd said earlier. I could sense he wanted to talk about it, so I asked about his mother. He repeated that they'd lost her in Katrina. She was already ill at Memorial Medical Center in New Orleans when Katrina arrived. The first floor of the hospital flooded, then the hospital lost power. The emergency generator flooded too. So all life support machines became nonfunctional. The hospital staff requested helicopter evacuations for their very ill patients, but they were denied for days. Temperatures in the building reached 110 degrees. Supplies were running out and doctors became desperate. Later, one of the doctors accused another of euthanizing the sickest of the patients in those dismal days as they waited for help, and wondered when and if it would come. The man standing before me said his mother's death was still "undetermined," which meant the coroner had been unable to confirm if her death was due to natural causes or homicide.

I'd heard about this hospital and the suspicious deaths in the news. It was just one of the many horrific stories of Katrina. But I never expected that I would meet the family of one of those patients. I hadn't given much thought to how it must feel to know your parent or spouse died in those horrific circumstances. But now I saw it in this man's eyes and heard it in his voice -- he was a son who wanted justice for his mother. Even two years later, the pain was fresh enough that he and his father were still grappling with what happened. In that moment they were no longer just part of a tragic news story. And I was uncomfortably aware that before Katrina they had been average people like the rest of us. I felt blessed and honored to work on their house.

This man told me more about the day the flood swept through his neighborhood. He said they barely had enough time to get themselves and two of their dogs into the attic. There were three other dogs that he couldn't reach in time. He started to say more, then stopped. "I can't tell you the rest, because I'll start crying."

We changed the conversation to less serious subjects. And after a little while I went back in the house to do more work. I'd been gone for about ten minutes, but I didn't feel too guilty about it. I knew rebuilding their home was important, but listening was important too.

The other two volunteers and I talked as we worked. We shared our impressions of The Parish, the recovery process and all the great people we'd met. All of us were overwhelmed by how kind the residents were. The older man of the two residents brought us an article he'd seen in the newspaper. It warned that injuries from saws were on the rise in the area. He was concerned for us -- he didn't want us to get injured.

I'm convinced the caring attitude of residents was the primary factor that motivated volunteers to return to The Parish repeatedly. In the course of my visits, I met dozens of volunteers who'd planned to work there for a week and then decided to stay for months. I'd met at least half a dozen people who moved there to rebuild full-time. Many of them were recent college graduates, who decided to postpone their job searches and devote their energy to a more purposeful calling. They may have been dreaming of new cars or larger apartments, but spending time in St. Bernard reset their priorities.

We worked for most of the day and completed a decent amount of flooring. When we were done I wanted to take a drive to see if there'd been improvements since my last visit two months earlier. Each rebuilt home or reopened store brought hope for the overall recovery of The Parish. And I wondered if I should film some of it and post an update on The Parish online.

Before this trip I'd received an e-mail from a man in The Parish. He said he'd seen my videos on YouTube and appreciated them. But he wondered why I hadn't done more positive stories about The Parish. Why hadn't I shown some of the houses that had been restored? Initially, I was offended. I'd been doing my best to get help to The Parish by showing how much work still needed to be done. I was concerned that showing progress would paint too rosy of a picture. There were some great stories of renewal in The Parish -- Buck and Molly's house was one of them. But people around the country were starting to forget that much work still needed to be done. If they didn't know help was still needed, why would they come there to volunteer? I took his question personally, but I should have known better than that. My ego was very much in the way. And what I wished I could say back was less than charitable. I thought, "If you don't like the way I present it, why don't you get your own damn camera and make your own video?" But, of course, I didn't say that.

I didn't respond to his comment at first. But, after I had some time to mull it over, I realized he meant well. So I wrote to him, explaining my position. He wrote back, saying he understood. Then he told me he was one of the local firefighters who'd been stranded in The Parish after Katrina. They'd been left with the task of rescuing people from their attics and rooftops.

Well, I felt about two feet tall for having been annoyed by his comment about my videos. I'd read a book called *Firestorm* that was self-published by a local woman named Michelle Mahl Buuck. She had family members in The Parish fire department and her book detailed the ordeal they'd faced when the whole Parish flooded. It was a harrowing situation. They'd been responsible for saving hundreds of lives by patrolling neighborhoods in borrowed boats, and finding food for those they rescued. The flood had destroyed all the firefighters' homes and their families had been evacuated. They were stranded in The Parish with little to no contact with their families. But they overcame the adversity to save Parish residents. Now that I knew who he was, I respected this man's comment about my videos, knowing that he wanted to share positive views of The Parish even after all he'd been through personally.

I pulled out my copy of *Firestorm*. I remembered a lot of the firefighters had been mentioned by name in it. So I wanted to look for this man's name in the book to get a better idea of what his personal experience had been during the flood. I'd read the whole book before, but since I hadn't known any of the firefighters, the names hadn't registered with me. So I opened the book to a random page and, as God is my witness, his name was on the first page I saw. Then I scanned the book and discovered his name was only on three out of 300 pages. That meant there was only a 1% chance of opening up to a page that included his name.

All the fire stations in St. Bernard had flooded. By the time I visited in October, none of the stations had been completely repaired. Over two years after Katrina, many fire stations were being operated from trailers. The station closest to my sister's new house had also been struck by a tornado during the storm, and it was still deserted. And many of the firefighters were still rebuilding their own homes. I think anger is a pretty useless emotion most of the time. But it's hard not to feel outraged about the lack of help firefighters were getting there. Because it might be time to reevaluate how our country uses its resources if we're not supporting our rescue workers.

So on this visit, I filmed a couple of the destroyed and abandoned fire stations. I also filmed an abandoned strip mall with national chain stores that were still ungutted. I titled the video "Fire Stations and Businesses 2 Years After Katrina" and put it on YouTube. In some ways I felt bad, because once again I was showing destruction in The Parish. But I hoped it would bring them some help. And I posed this question in the video, "The United States can do better than this, can't we?"

When I finished reading *Firestorm* the first time I noticed something. I started seeing fire engines all the time. I'd see a fire engine, truck or firefighter every time I left my house and drove somewhere -- even if I only drove for a mile. Maybe they were always there and I just didn't notice before. But I kept seeing them constantly. Maybe it was a sign, maybe not. When we were little, my mother taught my sisters and me to make the sign of the cross every time we heard a siren. As I got older it became too embarrassing to do that, so instead I'd say a quick prayer for whomever the siren was for and the emergency workers involved. After reading *Firestorm*, I created a new ritual that borrows from the one my mother taught us. Each time I see a fire engine, truck or firefighter I say a quick prayer for all firefighters affected by Katrina. Some days it gets almost ridiculous because I'll see eight or ten fire trucks, all in different areas, in the span of about five minutes.

While I was in New Orleans that October, wildfires were raging in many parts of Southern California. Many of the people I met showed concern and asked if my home would be affected. I assured them it wouldn't since I live in Northern California. But I deeply appreciated that they'd been paying attention to what was happening in my state. My cousin was a firefighter in Southern California and firefighters all over our state were being sent to battle the blazes. Several of my relatives lived near the fires and reported the smell of smoke was thick in their neighborhoods.

I picked up a New Orleans Times Picayune newspaper and read this on the front page: "Wounded New Orleanians helped by the kindness of strangers two years ago are looking toward fire-ravaged Southern California with an urge to help." The article had quotes from leaders of various New Orleans non-profits who said their phone lines were swamped with people asking what they could do for California. It gave me a lump in my throat to read that because I knew most of the local people still hadn't completely recovered from Katrina, but still they were asking how they could help us.

On the way home I had a layover in Dallas. On my second flight I was seated next to a man from Oakland. He asked where I'd been traveling. He was interested in the work I'd done as a volunteer and asked a lot of questions. He said he'd wanted to take his teenage son to volunteer in New Orleans just after Katrina, but he hadn't followed through on those plans. He expressed his regret that they hadn't done something to help. But I told him there were still plenty of opportunities -- St. Bernard Parish could still use thousands of volunteers.

When we parted company, he thanked me for going to Louisiana to help. I told him it was absolutely unnecessary for him to thank me -- I was lucky to be able to go there. I still remembered how I felt two years earlier, when I wanted to go there so badly, but couldn't. And I knew there were other people, like this man, who still hadn't had the chance.

CHAPTER TWENTY-TWO

Just Showing Up

The first time Sandy and I went to New Orleans after Katrina, we didn't have much of a plan. We'd signed up with a large non-profit agency to work at a relief center in New Orleans. We'd planned to work there and, in our spare time, drive out to The Parish to see how it was doing. But three days before the trip, I called to confirm our plans and was told the center in New Orleans wouldn't be open on the days we were there. I was very frustrated by this, because I'd told them what days we were going to be there when we signed up. We were left with a slight predicament. We had flights we couldn't cancel, reservations at a guesthouse, lots of good intentions and no place to volunteer. So I went online and found a small grassroots organization that was operating a relief center in St. Bernard Parish. And that was how our journey began.

In St. Bernard Parish we didn't see many of the large well-known relief organizations. But we did see a number of small church groups and grassroots organizations providing desperately needed assistance. These small groups weren't encumbered by bureaucracy -- they just showed up and helped.

These groups came from all faiths and all walks of life. Two of the biggest contributors in the early months were PRC Compassion (a conservative faith-based group) and Emergency Communities (also known as "the hippy camp" because many of the volunteers were young liberals who wore tie-dye clothing). These two groups from seemingly opposite backgrounds worked for a common purpose -- providing comfort and care to disaster survivors.

People in The Parish didn't really concern themselves with the belief systems of those relief workers. They were just happy that anyone cared enough to travel there and help out. As Sandy and I worked at the PRC Compassion center, many of the residents asked, "How did you know about us? What made you come here?"

We tried our best to help with rebuilding. But sometimes I think the most important things we did were meeting people, hearing their stories, learning of the challenges they faced and the faith they had. Because when a disaster happens, people need help with their physical needs. But what they need even more is to be seen and acknowledged and to know that someone cares.

And that thought is validated when I think of all the gratitude we received from people we never physically helped. They extended so many offers of help, food and discounts that it's hard to remember everything. But the overall lesson we took away was that it didn't matter to them what we did, they were just grateful that we were willing to do something.

When we arrived three months after Katrina, the owners of the guesthouse we stayed in couldn't stop thanking us for coming. We spent the first hour listening to them recount their terrifying experience of being trapped in New Orleans as floodwater overtook their city and chaos ensued. They kept telling us we were wonderful people for coming. "You're just like Oprah," they said. In our return visits they always went the extra mile to welcome us. They gave us discount rates on the room, brought us sparkling water, fresh fruit and boxes of candy. And attached to these gifts were handwritten notes that always included the words, "We love you." On later visits they gave each of us earrings and bracelets, and all they asked was that we think of them when we wore the jewelry. They did all these wonderful things for us simply because we came there when their community was in need. We didn't help the guesthouse owners rebuild -- we just listened to them.

And there is a lesson in all of this that I don't want to forget, because it can be applied to so many situations in life. So I need to remind myself that when a friend is going through a hard time, the best thing I can do is show up, even if I don't know what to do. In our society, we like to write checks to show our concern, and money can provide a great deal of relief. But it seems the gift that is often appreciated the most is the gift of our time.

In St. Bernard Parish, people who volunteered with non-profits like Emergency Communities and PRC Compassion gave that gift. And so did people like Zack Rosenberg and Liz McCartney, founders of The St. Bernard Project, who uprooted their comfortable lives to devote all their time to rebuilding The Parish.

Parish residents gave that gift too. They helped each other rebuild their homes and maintained the yards of friends who'd temporarily moved away. I remember seeing a man and woman mowing the grass and whacking the weeds on the neutral ground in their neighborhood. Many residents volunteered at the relief centers too. And The Parish government organized groups of locals to gut homes and restore parks. They all showed they cared by showing up for each other.

CHAPTER TWENTY-THREE

It Couldn't Hurt to Ask

Going to Louisiana alone made me realize how much I missed being there with Sandy. We hadn't been on a trip there together for nine months -- probably the longest stretch since Katrina.

As usual, I was antsy to get back there as soon as I got home to California. I started campaigning to get Sandy to go back with me. But she's always busy, and her calendar fills up quickly. A weekend with her usually must be scheduled months in advance. After just a little persuading, she laid out her schedule for me. "I can do it the last weekend of January." Problem. I had a schedule conflict of my own. "The only other weekend I have free in the near future would be the first weekend of February," she said. That weekend worked for me.

But when we looked at New Orleans' calendar of events our hopes dropped. The first weekend of February would be Mardi Gras weekend. It was already December. Most people book their rooms a year in advance for Mardi Gras. We'd never get a room. But we decided it couldn't hurt to ask. In hindsight, I think that should be the motto for all my post-Katrina endeavors.

I called Jay at our absolute favorite guesthouse. He was at a party when he answered his cell phone. I said, "Jay, I know it's ridiculous to even be asking, but do you have any rooms available at all for Mardi Gras?" I couldn't believe his answer, "Well actually, yes, I do. As a matter of fact, I have your favorite room with the balcony overlooking Bourbon Street available. The same person has had a standing reservation for that room for the past 12 years, but he called recently to say he couldn't make it this year. I'd love to rent it out to you girls. It'd make me much happier than renting to a stranger."

Sandy said it must be a sign -- we were meant to go. Who finds a reservation on Bourbon Street seven weeks before Mardi Gras? I quickly mailed a check to Jay to hold the room and booked a flight.

We made plans for what we'd do there. Sandy was in favor of making it a celebration weekend. Maybe we should bypass the volunteer work for a change. But I didn't know if I could do it. It might not feel right going all the way there and doing nothing to help.

She set me straight. "It used to be that the *only* reason we went there was to have fun. Are you saying you'll never be able to do that again? Is New Orleans always going to be a place where you have to work now?" She had a point.

Before Katrina I never cared about Mardi Gras. I thought it would be too crowded, too expensive. I'd rather go when it was less hectic. But I changed my mind when I saw Anderson Cooper on CNN, standing in the French Quarter for the first post-Katrina Mardi Gras. Now Mardi Gras was a symbol of New Orleans' recovery. If people around the country would still flock to the city for a party, they must believe the city was coming back. Katrina's damage had been a huge reminder of just how much some of us love that place, and how sad we'd be if it were gone. I put Mardi Gras at the top of my list of Things To Do Before I Die.

One morning, about a month before this conversation with Sandy, I put on my "Geaux Saints" t-shirt and went to the grocery store. At the register, the clerk noticed my shirt and asked if I was from New Orleans. I told him I wasn't, but I go there a lot. He said, "I've always wanted to go to Mardi Gras."

"I really want to go someday too," I responded. But a pang hit me. I wondered if I'd still be saying those words in 10 years.

So, I told Sandy she was right. I could do Mardi Gras -- just Mardi Gras -- with no regrets. I knew no one in Louisiana would hold it against me. Everyone I'd met there relished the city's reputation for fun. They were looking forward to the day when Mardi Gras, not Katrina, would once again be their primary claim to fame.

Sandy called Molly and gave her the news. Molly was excited and immediately made plans to schedule time off of work while we were there. We decided she should stay with us at our guesthouse for one night, so the three of us could party in The Quarter together. She told me, "I've never experienced Mardi Gras in The Quarter before." I was surprised -- she'd lived in the area her whole life. But she explained that her parents wouldn't allow it when she was young, and then she had children of her own. They'd gone to the parades in the Uptown district many times, but had never joined the party in The Quarter. She was looking forward to sharing the experience with us.

I told a friend how our last minute Mardi Gras plans had come together and she said, "It was meant to be. Something important is going to happen while you're there."

A few weeks later, we were in New Orleans and Mardi Gras turned out to be even more fun than I'd anticipated. The stories

I'd heard of women lifting their shirts were exaggerated. Sure, there were a few of those women. But most of the revelry was rated PG-13. The crowds were huge, but friendly. We heard it was the first post-Katrina crowd to rival the pre-Katrina numbers.

Sandy and I took a cab straight from the airport to the parade route, where Buck and Johnny took our suitcases and packed them in a car. The four of us found Molly and watched the parades for hours. It was a great vantage point. The stand was so high we could look straight into the eyes of people riding the floats. They were so close, they practically handed beads to us. We caught so many beads that we started collecting them in big bags that rested by our feet.

In the evening Molly, Sandy and I went to The Quarter to watch the crowds and catch more beads. Contrary to popular belief, you don't have to show your goodies to get beads -- especially during Mardi Gras. There was such an abundance of them that piles accumulated in the street, and we slipped and slid on them as we walked.

Sandy and I wanted to initiate Molly into our Hurricane ritual before we turned in for the night. So we walked to Lafitte's Blacksmith Shop and ordered three of the drinks. The bartender asked how we knew each other, so we told him the story of the day Sandy and I went looking for the oil spill zone and found Molly. We shared that we'd been so impressed by her positive attitude. Molly told him that we'd quickly become friends, "and now we're just like family." It was so true.

The next day Buck picked us up and we all went to The Parish to check on Sandy's house and pick up lunch at Ben's Pizza. The Parish was looking better every time we saw it, even though many houses and businesses still needed to be rebuilt. The good news was that residents were feeling more confident about coming back. And volunteers were showing up in respectable numbers.

On Fat Tuesday Sandy and I watched the Rex and Zulu parades and caught even more beads. We walked down Bourbon Street to watch the crowds and then down Royal Street to take in all the great costumes people were wearing. It was like a great big grown-up Halloween party that began at 8:00 in the morning. We spent the whole day laughing. And everywhere we went people greeted us with, "Happy Mardi Gras!" Jay, our favorite guesthouse owner said, "Just think, everywhere else in the country it's just Tuesday." Looking around at the sea of smiling silly people around us, it was hard to imagine that everyone at home was having an ordinary day. We went up to our balcony on the third floor and, even from that distance, the sound of the crowd on the street was a low roar.

For a long time I'd wanted to visit Frenchmen Street, because I'd heard it was a favorite stomping ground for locals. So in the evening, Sandy and I took a walk there. It was the scene of a giant street party. Music was playing and crowds of people were dancing in the street. Sandy and I joined the fun. In one corner a woman juggled fire batons. And an unmanned pick-up truck slowly hobbled down the road as a group of 20-somethings danced in the truck's bed.

It was getting late and we still hadn't had dinner. We found a restaurant that was full of people but the doors were locked. It was well past the restaurant's regular closing time. We went to the door and made pitiful faces until a host opened it. He said he could get us in if we'd be willing to share a table. No problem there, we were starving. So he asked around inside until he found a party willing to share space with us. He let us in and seated us with two women who were also sisters. They were from Pennsylvania, but they'd purchased a condo in New Orleans together as a home away from home. The four of us gabbed about our enthusiasm for the city and none of us could understand how anyone could feel differently. One of the sisters said, "New Orleans is a place you either love or hate. You either get it or you don't get it." The two of them were about 10 years older than Sandy and me, and I couldn't help feeling as if I were getting a glimpse into the future as we talked with them.

We'd been told that the police and the street cleaners ride through The Quarter at midnight and announce that Mardi Gras is over. Then everyone is supposed to go back to their rooms, and the bars are supposed to close. I asked Jay if the bars really do close. He said some of them stay open behind their closed doors and shutters. We wanted to see the closing down ceremony, so Sandy and I walked back to The Quarter. We figured it'd be fun to close out the night at The Blacksmith Shop again. The bartender who'd been serving when we were with Molly was there again and he remembered us.

Then a familiar face appeared in the doorway. It was a man we'd met in this same place on our first trip to New Orleans after Katrina. He was a city employee but he was from St. Bernard Parish. During our first meeting he'd told us his house had been destroyed and he was sleeping in a horse trailer. But when we expressed concern over his living situation he protested, "But it's a *nice* horse trailer." He didn't want us to feel sorry for him and he was counting his blessings. He thought things could be much worse. Over two years later we were all here again. We told him we remembered him from the early months after Katrina and described what he'd told us then. When we mentioned the horse trailer he protested again, "But it was a *nice* horse trailer." That was one of the things I loved most about people from this area. Even when a situation looked dismal, they still looked for the bright side.

It was getting close to midnight and the staff at The Blacksmith Shop started shooing the customers out. The bartender looked at Sandy and me and told us we didn't have to rush out, since we were unofficial St. Bernardians. But Sandy was tired and ready to call it a night.

We watched from the sidewalk outside the guesthouse as the police swept through the street, announcing it was time for everyone to go home. But the street cleaners weren't there this time. The crowd dwindled, but some of the clubs were still pumping out music. I tried to convince Sandy to stay out with me. But the only thing she wanted was a comfortable bed and a good night's sleep. I did not want to call it a night. The next morning we'd be flying home and Mardi Gras would be over.

We went inside and Sandy quickly fell asleep, but I couldn't -- I didn't want it to end. I was looking forward to being home with my family again, but I didn't want to leave New Orleans. I was like Cinderella at the ball and the clock was striking twelve. I couldn't get the words to the chorus of Aerosmith's song "I Don't Want to Miss a Thing" out of my head. Is it possible to love a place with as much intensity as you love a person? Absolutely. Especially when what you love most about being there is meeting the local people.

I decided to write in my journal while the memories of Mardi Gras were still fresh in my mind. And then the most beautiful thunderstorm flashed and boomed overhead. I could hear sheets of rain pounding against the window. And I didn't want to just watch it -- I wanted to be a part of it. So I stepped out on the balcony and let the rain soak through my clothes while the sky above me illuminated and darkened. Down the street, music was still blasting and people were still partying. But on that balcony I was alone with New Orleans, and everything was perfect.

I have a dream that someday I'll have a condo in The Quarter or a modest home in The Parish. And I'll hug everyone who ever helped rebuild Louisiana. I'll attend all the local celebrations and I'll learn to make the best Cajun and Creole foods. And if you meet me there I'll ask, "Where y'all from?" And then I'll invite you over for a shrimp boil and the best jambalaya you've ever tasted.

CHAPTER TWENTY-FOUR

Coming Home

A few months after Mardi Gras, summer arrived and the third anniversary of Katrina was just around the corner. St. Bernard's residents were still waiting for the MRGO to be closed. The Army Corps of Engineers estimated the job would be completed before the 2009 hurricane season, but they'd have to make it through the current hurricane season first.

Levees were breaching at an alarming rate along the Mississippi River, flooding towns in the Midwest. It looked as though the Army Corps of Engineers would have its hands full for the next few years. St. Bernardians and New Orleanians watched the news coverage of the floods in the Midwest with empathy in their hearts. The scenes of flood-damaged homes looked all too familiar. They knew exactly how it felt to come home to water damage and black mold. And I wondered how many other towns might be underwater -- towns that most of us would never know about. And I hoped someone would find them.

In St. Bernard Parish, progress marched on in ways that brought both joy and sadness. Roughly a quarter of the homes had been demolished. One fourth of the homes gone! I tried to imagine how it would feel to drive through neighborhoods in my own city and see a quarter of the houses missing. In St. Bernard, residents who had rebuilt watched as their neighbors' homes were knocked down. Houses that had been part of The Parish landscape for thirty years were reduced to rubble in a matter of minutes.

Businesses were returning slowly but surely -- grocery stores, restaurants and clothing stores made life a little easier. The signs of progress encouraged people who'd moved away, and more of them were returning. Most had finally received the funds that had been promised shortly after the flood – even though it took about a year and a half for the first checks to arrive.

In July I called The Parish President's office to ask how many people had returned. They forwarded my call to The Parish's local Homeland Security Office. The representative said about 32,500 residents had returned to The Parish. That was about half the number of people who'd lived there before Katrina. The Homeland Security representative and I talked for a moment about how much progress had been made there since the early months. I told him I'd been there three months after

Katrina and he asked where I'd worked. When I said I'd been at the relief center in the Wal-Mart Parking lot he said, "Oh, thank you so much! We just can't thank the volunteers enough. When you come back to The Parish the next time, stop in at the government complex and say hi." And despite everything I'd learned, I was still surprised by how friendly everyone was in The Parish.

The St. Bernard Project estimated that over 6000 people from twelve countries had volunteered through their program alone. They'd helped rebuild 140 homes. But more families were still in need of help. After all, this was a community where 27,000 homes had been destroyed. I knew there were still people in our country that longed to contribute. Maybe they were feeling discouraged by circumstances that prevented them from traveling there, just as I had been back in 2005.

But in time they would find The Parish, and the locals would welcome them with hugs and freshly boiled crawfish. They'd see the parades and the determination on the residents' faces. They'd build homes and friendships that would last a lifetime. And when they went home, they'd write in their journals and tell their friends that they had found inspiration in the aftermath. And then they'd make plans to go back.

"I was hungry and you fed me, thirsty
and you gave me drink;
I was a stranger and you invited me
into your homes..."

Matthew 25:35

SITES TO SEE

St. Bernard Parish Government Office

www.sbpg.net

The St. Bernard Project

www.stbernardproject.org

Wetlands Restoration & MRGO Closure

mrgomustgo.org

St. Bernard Parish Animal Shelter

SBPanimal.homestead.com

PRC Compassion

Prccompassion.net

The New Orleans Times-Picayune

www.nola.com

VIDEOS OF ST. BERNARD PARISH

Guerra Family Video After Hurricane Katrina

Filmed by a survivor as he waited for help on his roof

www.youtube.com/askwestley

Dog and Cat Adoptions in St. Bernard Parish

www.youtube.com/missboomer

Videos Taken by J Baker Young:

House That Floated Down the Street

Fire Stations and Businesses 2 Years After Katrina

St. Bernard Parish Animal Shelter

Councilman Mark Madary

www.youtube.com/calivolunteer

Beyond New Orleans - St. Bernard Parish One Year After

Katrina on Google Videos

RECOMMENDED READING

Firestorm by Michelle Mahl Buuck

Xlibris Corporation

Lost In Katrina by Mikel Schaefer

Pelican Publishing Company

1 Dead in Attic by Chris Rose

Chris Rose Books

For more information or to order more copies of Nothing But Love: A Katrina Volunteer Finds Inspiration in the Aftermath, visit my web site at www.All4Won.com

www.ingramcontent.com/pod-product-compliance
Lightning Source LLC
Chambersburg PA
CBHW031625160426
43196CB00006B/287